Fred Parks'

LAS VEGAS

GUIDE TO
GAMING & FUN

7 Games | 7 Wins

Table of Contents

PAGES

Introduction   8 - 9

What to expect from this book and a special thanks to the people who helped me with the contents.

Las Vegas Facts   10 - 17

Facts about Las Vegas, when it started, people who live here and what the future holds for this area.

Places To Visit   18 - 21

Places of interest to visitors and suggestions of places I know you will enjoy.

Restaurants Of Distinction   22 - 23

Specialty restaurants you will enjoy. A brief outline of the kind of cuisine prepared at each location.

Hotel-Casino Listing   24 - 27

Listing of all major hotel-casinos with their telephone numbers.
Taxicabs and limousines are listed with telephone numbers.

Table of Contents cont.

Las Vegas Tipping Guide   28 - 30

Tipping or tokes are a way of life in Las Vegas. I list the best toke for the service, to get the best service.

Bingo Guide   31 - 33

List of all Las Vegas Bingo sessions, their addresses and the times of play.

Sports Book Guide   34 - 36

Not all hotels-casinos have a sports book to place bets on sporting events. We list the sportbooks and the time they open.

Golf Course Guide   38 - 41

Visitors that want to relax while in Las Vegas will find many fine golf courses on which to play. We give you the course, address, telephone number and if it is public or at a resort.

Table of Contents cont.

Map Of Casino Locations   42

A map of down-town and the strip are given to enable you to find the location you want to travel to.

Gaming   43 - 47

Gaming is big business. We want you to know the facts on gaming before presenting the games to you. Read this chapter before study ing the games.

Baccarat   48 - 60

A list of terminology for Baccarat is given for you to study before playing the game. I give you a recommended play-guide to make you a winner.

Blackjack (21)   61 - 74

Terminology is given for terms used in Black-jack. Money management for Blackjack is given. Recommended play for each hand is given. Double-down, splits, surrender, insurance, I explain each of these to you and how to play accordingly. A map for all plays is given.

Table of Contents cont.

Craps (Dice)   75 - 86

Terminology is given for language used in craps. Recommended play is given for every type of bet available on the Craps' lay-out or table. Follow our suggested play and be a winner.

Keno   87 - 96

Keno is available in every casino, in their restaurants, gaming areas, clubs, bars, or your resting area. Know how to place a bet, how to write a ticket, and how to figure your winnings before a bet is placed. Read our recommended play suggestions before you write your first ticket.

Poker   97 - 108

Las Vegas poker is usually limited to Texas Holdem and 7 Card Stud. I define these two games for you, giving recommended play for each. Not every casino has a poker room, a list of the casinos and the games featured with the stakes involved (High, Medium, Low) is in cluded in this section.

Table of Contents cont.

Roulette   109 - 116

A relaxing game that can be played to win. My terminology is given to let you understand the game before beginning play. My recommended play is the best ever.

Video Poker (Slots) Machines   117 - 124

What machine should you look for, how to play it to win. Terminology used in play of the machines. Read this chapter before trying your skill or luck at the rows of machines in every casino. Our recommended play will make you a winner.

Grand Finale   125 - 126

File Information   127

Introduction

Let me introduce you to LAS VEGAS by explanation of places to see, places to dine, casinos and games of chance.

I dedicate this book to all who have visited LAS VEGAS without a game plan on where to go, where to dine, location of casinos, or a plan on how to play the games. My book will enlighten you on these aspects of LAS VEGAS, to let you have fun and hopefully a profitable visit. We cannot make you a professional game player, but will give you knowledge to play the games without throwing your money away. Most visitors come to LAS VEGAS without knowledge of the games, and/or their rules. They just want the experience of LAS VEGAS gaming. Read my book, plan on visiting some of the places I recommend, dine at some of the best restaurants in the world and play the games according to my game plan given for each game. No one can make you a winner, except you. Plan for it, study for it, do it in a manner you can go home and brag about - be a WINNER.

As a graduate of International School of Gaming, Las Vegas, I dedicate this book to those souls that will be serving you in gaming. They have studied hard, practiced hard, and are ready to work hard at giving you their best at the games of your pleasure. The instructors who have taken time to assist me in writing this book, I say a special thanks.

Thanks gang, for letting me pass through your life. Sincerely,

Fred E. Parks

CHAPTER 1

Las Vegas, Nevada

L as Vegas became a town in 1905, when the Union created Water Hole No. 2 and permanent structures were built. Early development was rapid and property covenants written to make drinking and gambling legal. The first downtown hotel-casino was built in 1940 and still operating as the EL CORTEZ on 6th and Fremont. The strip wasn't a reality until after World War II. None of the early hotels could hold a candle to todays Strip hotels or those on Fremont Street, but they were the beginnings of America's renowned gaming city. The results are the "Entertainment Capitol of the world - LAS VEGAS".

Las Vegas (Clark County) has a population of 590,600 that live here year round. We have another 100,000 that live here for 3 or 4 months then move on to other parts. We have another 200,000 that come in for 3 to 4 days just to enjoy themselves. Another 30,000 come here to stay every year. Added all together, we have almost one (1) million people here every night and day of the year. Visitors soon discover what residents have always known, nowhere else in the world does eye-popping dazzle of the entertainment capitol of the world blend so well with opportunities for year round family recreational pursuits and a growing retirement community of affluent seniors.

Las Vegas area has sunshine 88 percent of the year. Daily average temperature is 80 degrees and average minimum is 54 degrees. Rainfall is infrequent with only 1.27 inches falling in 1985. Snow rarely falls in the Las Vegas area and melts as it falls or soon thereafter. The four seasons are well defined. Winters are mild and pleasant (daytime temperatures average 60 degrees), summers display desert conditions (temperatures average in 100 degree range). Spring and Fall seasons are ideal. There are very few days during the spring and fall months that outdoor activities are affected by the weather.

Lake Mead has six marinas that provide boat ramps, rentals for sailing, house-boating, power boating and water skiing. There are several beaches at the lake for sunning and swimming. Overnight lodging is provided at several marinas. Canoeing and rafting on the Colorado River are very popular.

Fishermen come from all parts of the world to fish for largemouth bass, striper and catfish in Lake Mead, Lake Mohave and the Colorado River. Water sports are big in the LAS VEGAS area year round. Other water sports include scuba diving, sailboating, and hydrotubing.

Thirteen golf courses, several of championship caliber are located in the LAS VEGAS area. There are five tennis clubs and many public tennis courts for the outdoors sports person.

Just 35 miles north of Las Vegas is Mount Charleston recreation area. It offers winter sports and relief from the summer heat. With the Toiyabe National Forest camp-grounds, lodge, hiking trails, winter ski slopes and other out-doors recreation ac-tivities, the Mount Charleston area offers a break from the hot desert floor in Las Vegas.

LAS VEGAS, known as the "Entertainment Capitol of the World", has all types of entertainment acts performing every night. They have superstars, lavish stage spectaculars, cabarea shows, and the drive down Las Vegas Blvd. at night is a sight to see. No wonder traffic is heavy with people driving and looking up.

Many of Las Vegas hotel-casinos provide entertainment for the family. The Imperial Palace's auto collection, Ceasars Palace's Omnimax Theatre, Hilton's Youth Hotel, and live circus acts at Circus Circus Hotel-Casino. Other places providing family entertainment are Wct-N-Wild Water Park, Ripley's Believe It or Not Museum, Old Mormon Fort, and UNLV Natural History Museum. Most important, don't forget to visit Hoover Dam. This is a sight all should see. Your time will be well spent in visiting the dam and the Hoover Dam area.

Las Vegas convention facilities are second to none. The Las Vegas Convention Center has facilities to accommodate 87,000 people at one time. Add all the convention facilities at the hotels and Las Vegas has room to accomodate 250,000 people any single day.

Las Vegas has 60,000 hotel-motel rooms available every night. Add the many time-share apartments, day-week apartments, mobile camps and people staying with family and friends, you can see where all 200,000 visitors have rooms to stay in Las Vegas every night. Las Vegas Hilton with 3174 rooms and suites is Las Vegas's largest hotel-casino at this time.

Some of the large convention events are American Bowling Congress, Las Vegas Silver Cup Hydroplane Race, National Finals Rodeo, Consumers Electronic Show, and AMD/ASD Trade Show. Add many smaller shows each year and you can see why Las Vegas is the trade convention center of the world.

Nellis Air Force Base has more than 12,000 military and civilian personnel working, making it the single largest employer in Nevada. Add 35,000 family members and 11,000 military retirees, the

Nellis community has over 60,000 people to add to the Las Vegas population. Out of state visitors to Nellis add 25,000 to the ranks of visitors of Las Vegas every month.

Las Vegas is fast becoming the retirement area of our nation. One out of six residents of Las Vegas is retired. That counts up to 116,000 making Las Vegas their retirement home. Reasons for retiring here are many: Weather, reasonable living expenses, recreation facilities, travel facilities (airport has 657 flights daily) and taxes.

Nevada Taxes: Gasoline 13¢ plus 5¢ Clark County per gallon

Personal Income Tax	None
Inheritance-gift taxes	None
Property Tax	Limited
Sales-Use Tax	6 percent, food exempt

IN THE FUTURE - A super speed train linking Southern California to Las Vegas in the mid 1990's traveling at 200 miles per hour. The Festival Market-Place downtown will create 200,000 square feet of visitor attractions. Plans for 25,000 single family homes are approved and waiting to be finished. All over the Las Vegas basin construction is going on, about to start, or in the planning stage. The New Golden Nugget will break ground soon and become the largest Hotel-Casino in the world (3500 rooms planned). The Japanese are investing heavily in this area. They now own the Aladdin Hotel-Casino and Dunes Hotel-Casino. They are investing in many other types of business in Nevada. Foreign investment is increasing, bringing many foreign visitors to our area wanting to see the entertainment capitol of the world "LAS VEGAS".

Del Webb's new Sun City in the planning stages will bring another 25,000 retirees to the Vegas area. This whole new city will bring many new businesses, people, investment and facilities to Las Vegas. By the year 2000 the total population of this area will exceed 1 million.

Las Vegas has always been known as the Divorce Capitol of the World, it may surprise you to know that there were 63,674 marriages performed in Las Vegas in 1986 compared to 8,997 divorces. There is no required waiting period or blood test. License cost $25 while ceremony fees vary depending on the Wedding Chapel. The most popular wedding days are New Year's Eve and Valentine's Day.

CHAPTER 2

Las Vegas - Places To Visit

Bally's Grand Theatre Bally Hotel-Casino
See the Las Vegas style of watching great classic movies in the comfort of a Hollywood screening room. Your own personal cocktail waitress - comfortable two-seat couches. Located in Bally's Hotel-Casino. Call for showtimes 739-4111.

Binion's Horseshoe Hotel-Casino 128 Fremont Blvd. Have your picture made with a million dollars. Daily from 12 pm til 12 am.

Circus Circus Hotel 2880 So. Las Vegas Blvd. A variety of games for the entire family on 2nd floor - while watching exciting free circus acts from 11 am to 12 pm. Win prizes or have a pizza in a carnival atmosphere.

Ethel M's Candy Mt. Vista Road - Henderson
Manufacturing Plant

See this modern plant preparing the finest in chocolates. Phone 458-8864 for tour information.

Hoover Dam - Lake Mead   Hwy. 93 East, 25 Miles
Visit the largest man-made lake in the world. Hoover Dam holds back the Colorado River to form this wonder. Tours daily from 8 am to 6:30 pm.

Imperial Palace Auto Collection 3535 So. Las Vegas Blvd.
Over 200 antique cars on display. Cars owned by Al Capone, President Eisenhower, and Hitler are on display. Open daily 9:30 am to 11:30 pm.

Wet N Wild   So. Las Vegas Blvd.
This family water park has 26 acres of water fun with 15 attractions including 76-foot Der Stuka vertical drop water slide. Open daily 10 am til 8 pm.

Ripley's Believe It or Not Museum   Fremont Blvd.
(4 Queens Hotel)
Displays over 1,000 unbelievable, fascinating items in this museum of incredible detail and imagination. Open daily 9 am to 12 midnight.

Red Rock Canyon   5 miles west on Charleston Blvd. Scenic drive through the wonderous red rock formations of southern Nevada. The scenic belt loop takes you past 15 miles of beautiful desert scenery.

Mt. Charleston   45 miles north Hwy. 95 to Reno Get back to nature at Mt. Charleston that offers hiking, camping as well as a hotel and two restaurants/lodges. Escape the city heat.

Olde Tyme Gambling Museum   So. Las Vegas Blvd. (Stardust Hotel-Casino) Features antique slots, gambling devices, Americana collectibles and displays unique to gaming. Daily 9 am to 1 am.

Liberace Museum & Foundation 1775 E. Tropicana Ave. Famous entertainer Liberace's former home now a show place and museum.

Sam's Town Hotel-Casino   5111 Boulder Hwy. The old time ice-cream parlor is a fancy to all ages.

Las Vegas Blvd.   from Fremont Street South
A drive down this street at night is something no-one
will forget. The signs, people, structures-buildings
and many sights no-one can describe will fill your
hour drive time.

CHAPTER 3

Las Vegas Restaurants of Distinction

Andre's   385-5016   401 South 6th
French cuisine at its best.

Alpine Village   734-6888   3003 Paradise Road
Swiss-German food in old world charm.

Battista's
Hole in the
Wall   732-1424   4041 Audrie
Italian food in Italian atmosphere.

Cafe Michelle   735-8686   1350 East Flamingo
Original sidewalk cafe - featuring continental
cuisine.

Chicago Joe's   382-5246   820 South 4th
Italian dishes and seafood.

Chinese Garden   876-5432   5485 West Sahara Ave.
Cantonese dining in Chinese atmosphere.

Olive Garden   735-0082   1545 East Flamingo
Totally Italian - totally excellent.

Philips Supper
House   873-0082   4545 West Sahara Ave.
Famous for Prime Rib and Angus Steaks.

Sandpiper   458-5555   3311 E. Flamingo Rd.
Finest selection of seafood featuring - abalone -Maine Lobsters.

State Street   733-0225   2570 State St.
Finest of dining featuring steaks, seafood, prime rib.

We did not mention the many fine selections of dining that can be found in all of the major hotel-casinos. Each hotel features at least one dining experience you will be proud to have. Ask your bell-captain in the hotel you are staying to recommend one for you to satisfy your taste.

CHAPTER 4

Las Vegas - Hotels

Aladdin Hotel 736-0111

Alexis Park 796-3300

Bally's.. 739-4111

Barbary Coast 737-7111

Binion's Horseshoe 382-1600

Bourbon Street 737-7200

Caesars Palace 731-7110

California Hotel 385-1222

Circus Circus 734-0410

Continental Hotel 737-5555

Desert Inn 733-4444

Dunes Hotel 737-4110

El Cortez 385-5200

El Rancho 796-2222

Flamingo Hilton.............................. 733-3111

Four Queens................................. 385-4011

Fremont Hotel 385-3232

Frontier Hotel 734-0110

Golden Gate................................. 382-6300

Golden Nugget 385-7111
Gold Coast 367-7111
Gold Spike 384-8444
Hacienda Hotel 739-8911
Holiday Casino 369-5000
Imperial Palace 731-3311
Jerry's Nugget 399-3000
Lady Luck Hotel 384-4680
La Mirage 733-7777
Landmark Hotel 733-1110
Las Vegas Club 385-1664
Las Vegas Hilton 732-5111
Las Vegas Inn 731-3222
Mardi Gras Inn 731-2020
Marina Hotel 739-1500
Maxim Hotel 731-4300
Mint Hotel 387-6468
Nevada Palace 458-8810
Paddlewheel 734-0711
Palace Station 367-2411
Pioneer Club 386-5000
Riviera Hotel 734-5110

Royal Las Vegas 735-6117
Sahara Hotel 737-2111
Sam's Town 456-7777
Sands Hotel 733-5000
Showboat Hotel 385-9123
Silver City 732-4152
Silver Nugget 399-1111
Silver Slipper 734-1212
Stardust Hotel 732-6111
Sundance Hotel(Fitzgerald) 382-6111
Tropicana Hotel 739-2222
Union Plaza 386-2110
Vegas World 382-2000
Viscount Hotel 735-1167
Western Hotel 384-4620
Westward Ho 731-2900

TAXICABS

A-North Las Vegas 643-1041
A Vegas Western 736-6121
ABC Union 736-8444
Ace Cab 736-8383

TAXICABS cont.

Checker 873-2227

Desert Cab 736-1702

Nellis Cab 798-1149

Star Cab......................................736-2227

Western Cab 736-8000

Whittlesea...................................384-6111

Yellow 873-2227

LIMOUSINES

Bell 736-4428

Desert Limo 383 5883

Las Vegas Limo 739-8414

Longride Limo 735-5211

Lucky 7 Luxury Limo 739-6177

Presidential Limo.........................731-5577

Trans Cont Ind 734-1166

CHAPTER 5

Las Vegas Tipping Guide

Tipping is a custom based on the generosity of an appreciative customer, and therefore is subject to no concrete rules. Here are a few suggestions as what to give for service rendered.

Matra'D: To get the best seat in the house at a show, tip the Matra'd the price of one seat - party of four. If less than 4, accordingly.

Showroom Waiters: $5 - $10 for a party of 2 - 4, cocktail show only. Dinner show depending on service and quality of food $10 - $20.

Restaurant Waiters: Usually 15 - 20 percent of bill.

Valet Parking: $1 standard, $2 if extra service given such as open doors, quick service, etc.

Bellman: $2 - $5 depending on need for his service during your stay.

Room Service: Standard 15 - 20 percent applies.

Bartenders: $1 per round for parties of 2 - 4, more for larger groups.

Cocktail Waitresses: $1 a round for parties of 2 - 4, more for groups.

Dealers: Tips or tokes as they are called, can be given directly to the dealer or you may place a bet or wager for the dealer. If you win a Blackjack while playing 21, the $1 to $5 toke on the next hand will get you a dealer looking out for you. Playing craps, winning a long roll of the dice, placing a toke bet for the dealers on 11 is greatly appreciated.

Bingo - Keno Runners: Generosity and conscience should guide big winners. If you are playing for an extended time, $1 every once-in-awhile, will be appreciated.

Pool Attendant: 50 cents to $1 for towels, cots, etc.

Skycaps: $1 for 1 - 4 pieces of luggage, more for extra service.

Taxicab Drivers: $1 to $2 for a direct route. More if extra service given.

Hotel Maids: $1.50 per day at the conclusion of your stay.

Remember most of these people have low-paying jobs, and the people who perform them rely on tips or tokes for their living. Treat these people with a smile and a tip, and you have a friend in Las Vegas.

CHAPTER 6

Las Vegas Bingo Guide

Continental
Hotel   737-5555 4100 Paradise Rd.
Session times:
9:30 am   11 am   1 pm   3 pm   5 pm   7 pm   11 pm

El Rancho   796-2222 2755 Las Vegas Blvd.
Session times:
10 am   12 pm   2 pm   4 pm   6 pm   8 pm   10 pm

Fremont   385-3232 200 East Fremont St.
Session times:
9:30 am 11 am 1 pm 3 pm 5 pm 7 pm 9 pm 11 pm

Gold Coast   367-7111 4000 West Flamingo
Session times:
10 am 12-noon 2 pm 4 pm 6 pm 8 pm 10 pm 12 pm

Holiday Inn   369-5232 3475 Las Vegas Blvd.
Session times:
1 pm3:30 pm7 pm9:30 pmContinuous 9:30 pm-1:30 am

Jerry's Nugget   399-3000 1821 Las Vegas Blvd.
Session times:
10:45 am 1 pm 3 pm 5 pm 7 pm 9 pm 11 pm 1 am

Nevada Palace   458-8810 5255 Boulder Hwy.
Session times:
(free bingo) 10 am   12 am   2 pm   7 pm   9 pm

Palace Station   367-2411 2411 West Sahara Ave.
Session times:
9:30 am 11 am 1 pm 3 pm 5 pm 7 pm 11 pm 1 am

Sam's Town   456-7777 5111 Boulder Hwy.
Session times:
9:30 am 11 am 1 pm 3 pm 5 pm 7 pm 9 pm 11 pm 1 am 2:45 am

Showboat   385-9123 2800 E. Fremont St.
Session times:
9:30 am 11 am 1 pm 3 pm 5 pm 7 pm 9 pm 11:45 pm 1:15 am

Silver Nugget   399-1111 2140 Las Vegas Blvd.
Session times:
9 am 11 am 1 pm 3 pm 5 pm 7 pm 9 pm 11 pm

Western Hotel   384-4620 499 East Fremont St.
Session times:
2 pm   8 pm   Continuous 9 am-6 pm

HENDERSON
Eldorado Club   564-1811 140 So. Water St.
Session times:
(free bingo) 9:30 am   (pay) 3:30 pm   7 pm   9:30 pm

Railroad Pass   294-5000 2800 Boulder Hwy.
Session times:
(free bingo)   Mon.-Thur.   9:30 am
(pay) 11 am   1 pm   3:30 pm   5:30 pm   7:30 pm

BOULDER CITY
Gold Strike   293-5000 U.S. Hwy. 93
Session times:
(free bingo) Mon.-Wed. 3 pm   (pay) 5 pm   7 pm   9 p
LAUGHLIN
Riverside   298-2535 1650 Casino Way
Session times:
8 am   10 am   12 pm   2 pm   4 pm   6 pm   8 pm   10 pm

CHAPTER 7

Las Vegas Sports Books Guide

Bally's   739-4111   3645 S. Las Vegas Blvd.
Race & Sports Book. Wagering on all major amateur and professional sports. Open 9 am to 9 pm. 24 hours on major sports weekends.

Caesar's Palace 731-7110   3570 S. Las Vegas Blvd.
Race & Sports Book. Open 8 am to 12 midnight. 24 hours on major events.

Circus Circus   734-0410   2880 S. Las Vegas Blvd.
Race & Sports Book. Open 8:30 daily until last race or event closes.

El Cortez Hotel 385-5200   600 E. Fremont
Sports Book. Open 8 am to 12 midnight daily.

Fremont Hotel 385-3232   200 E. Fremont
Race & Sports Book. Open 8:30 am until last race daily.

Frontier Hotel
& Casino   734-0110   3120 S. Las Vegas Blvd.
Race & Sports Book. Open daily 8:30 am to 8:30 pm.

Gold Coast Hotel
              367-7111   4000 W. Flamingo Rd.
Race & Sports Book. Open 24 hours daily.

Holiday Casino 369-5000   3473 S. Las Vegas Blvd.
Race & Sports Book. Open 24 hours daily.

Jerry's Nugget 399-3000   1821 N. Las Vegas Blvd.
Race & Sports Book. Open 9:30 am to 5:30 pm
Sat.-Sun.

Las Vegas Club 385-1664   18 Fremont St.
Sports Book. Open 9 am to 11 pm daily.

Las Vegas Hilton
              732-5111   3000 Paradise Rd.
Race & Sports Book. Open 24 hours daily.

Palace Station 367-2411   2411 W. Sahara Ave.
Race & Sports Book. Open 9 am to last game or race.

Riviera Hotel   734-5110   2901 S. Las Vegas Blvd.
Race & Sports Book. Open 24 hours daily.

Sahara Hotel   737-2111   2525 S. Las Vegas Blvd.
Race & Sports Book. Open 8:30 am until last game
or race.

Sams Town   456-7777   5111 Boulder Hwy.
Race & Sports Book. Open 9 am to 8 pm.

Sands Hotel   733-5000   3555 S. Las Vegas Blvd.
Race & Sports Book. Open daily 9 am to 11:30 pm.

Showboat Hotel 385-9123   2800 E. Fremont
Race & Sports Book. Open 8:30 am to 10:30 pm.

Tropicana   739-2222   3801 S. Las Vegas Blvd.
Race & Sports Book. Open 9 am to 9 pm daily.

CHAPTER 8

Las Vegas Golf Course, Tennis & Racquetball Courts Guide

GOLF COURSE GUIDE

Black Mountain Country Club
    Public   565-7933   501 Country Club Drive

Craig Rach Golf Course
    Public   642-9700   628 W. Craig Road

Desert Inn Country Club
    Resort   733-4444   Desert Inn Hotel

Desert Rose Golf Course
    Public   438-4653   5483 Club House Drive

Dunes Country Club
    Resort   734-4749   Dunes Hotel Casino

Las Vegas Municipal Golf Course
    Public   646-3003   Decatur & Washington

No Las Vegas Golf Course
    Public   649-7171   324 E. Brooks

Showboat Country Club
    Resort   451-2106   Showboat Hotel

Sahara Country Club
    Resort   796-0013   Sahara Hotel

Tropicana Country Club
    Resort   739-2579   Tropicana Hotel

TENNIS COURTS GUIDE

Aladdin Hotel-Casino
    Resort   736-0497   3667 S. Las Vegas Blvd.
    3 courts (lighted). Fees: Hotel guest free - $5/court
hour.

Alexis Park Hotel Casino
    Resort   796-3300   375 Harmon
    2 courts (lighted). Fees: Hotel guest none.

Bally's Hotel Casino

Resort   739-4111   3645 S. Las Vegas Blvd.

10 courts (lighted). Fees: Hotel guest none - $10 per person/court hour.

Caesar's Palace Hotel-Casino

Resort   731-7786   3570 S. Las Vegas Blvd.

6 courts (lighted). Fees: Hotel guest none - $5 per person/court hour.

Desert Inn Hotel Casino

Resort   733-4577   3145 S. Las Vegas Blvd.

10 courts (lighted). No court fees.

Dunes Hotel-Casino

Resort   737-4494   3650 S. Las Vegas Blvd.

5 courts (lighted). No court fees.

Flamingo Hilton Hotel-Casino

Resort   733-3344   3555 S. Las Vegas Blvd.

4 courts (lighted). Fees: $5 per court hour - Pro available.

Frontier Hotel Casino

Resort   734-0110   3120 S. Las Vegas Blvd.

2 courts (lighted). Fees: Hotel guest none - $5 per person/court hour.

Las Vegas Hilton Hotel-Casino

Resort   732-5111   3000 Paradise Road

6 courts (lighted). Fees: Hotel guest none. Teaching pro available.

Racket Club

Private   385-1193   98 Highland Ave.

6 courts (lighted). Private and group lessons available.

Sands Hotel Casino

Resort   733-5000   3355 S. Las Vegas Blvd.

6 courts (lighted). Fees: $2 per court hour/guest -$3 per hour/non-guest.

Union Plaza Hotel Casino

Resort   386-2110   1 Main St.

4 courts (lighted). Fees: Hotel guest none. Teaching pro available.

RACQUETBALL COURTS GUIDE

Caesars Palace Hotel Casino
       731-7110   3570 S. Las Vegas Blvd.
Court fees: $7 for 2 players/court hour.

The Sports Club
       733-8999   3025 Industrial Road
Court fees: $15 per person includes full use of the facility.

Las Vegas Athletic Club
       733-1919   1070 East Sahara Ave.
Guest fees: $7 per person/court hour. Includes full use of facility.

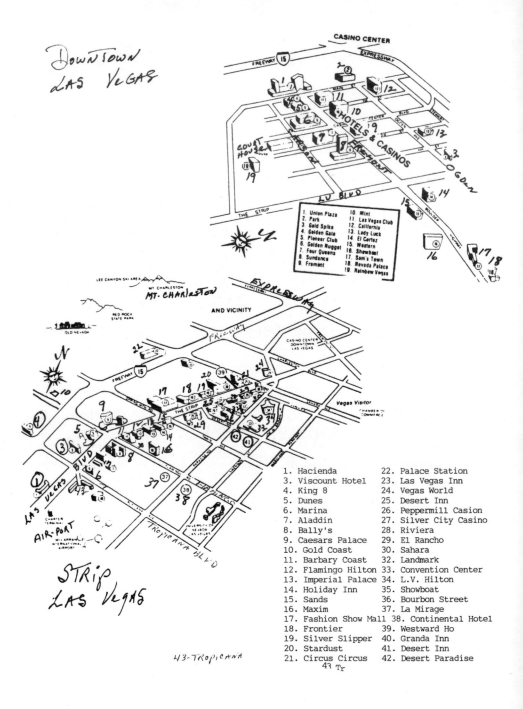

Downtown Las Vegas

CASINO CENTER

1. Union Plaza	10. Mint
2. Park	11. Las Vegas Club
3. Gold Spike	12. California
4. Golden Gate	13. Lady Luck
5. Pioneer Club	14. El Cortez
6. Golden Nugget	15. Western
7. Four Queens	16. Showboat
8. Sundance	17. Sam's Town
9. Fremont	18. Nevada Palace
	19. Rainbow Vegas

MT. CHARLESTON AND VICINITY

Strip Las Vegas

1. Hacienda	22. Palace Station
3. Viscount Hotel	23. Las Vegas Inn
4. King 8	24. Vegas World
5. Dunes	25. Desert Inn
6. Marina	26. Peppermill Casion
7. Aladdin	27. Silver City Casino
8. Bally's	28. Riviera
9. Caesars Palace	29. El Rancho
10. Gold Coast	30. Sahara
11. Barbary Coast	32. Landmark
12. Flamingo Hilton	33. Convention Center
13. Imperial Palace	34. L.V. Hilton
14. Holiday Inn	35. Showboat
15. Sands	36. Bourbon Street
16. Maxim	37. La Mirage
17. Fashion Show Mall	38. Continental Hotel
18. Frontier	39. Westward Ho
19. Silver Slipper	40. Granda Inn
20. Stardust	41. Desert Inn
21. Circus Circus	42. Desert Paradise

43-TROPICANA
43 Tr

42

CHAPTER 9

Gaming - Las Vegas Style

The gaming business in Nevada has increased at the rate of approximately 10% per year since 1980. Gaming revenues during 1986-87 as reported by the state of Nevada was $3.7 BILLION dollars. That means over $1 Billion dollars exchange hands in Nevada every day of the year, just from gaming. No wonder so many states are looking at gaming as a source of revenue. Even the Federal Government is looking at a national lottery to pay our huge national debt. Games authorized in states are:

Bingo .... 39 states
Horse racing .... 33 states
Lotteries .... 26 states
Dog racing .... 13 states
Numbers .... 8 states
Card rooms .... 7 states
Jai Alai .... 5 states
Sports Book .... 3 states
Off Track .... 2 states
Casino .... 2 states

Before we give you information on each game and Video-slot games, we want you to know that gaming is an adult play of games. We as adults hope to win money, but we really enjoy the action. Gambling fulfills our:

1. Need to feel alive,
2. Need to feel worthwhile, and
3. Gets us excited and aroused.

Gambling releases us from the real world. There is no outside, no past, or future. Only here and now. Our whole is based on the next card or roll of the dice. Before you start to gamble, you should have:

1. Knowledge of the game,
2. Independence of your thought and action,
3. Basic knowledge of odds in cards or dice,
4. Self control,
5. Game plan,
6. Experience,
7. Bankroll - gamble with money you can afford to lose.

8. Accumulate a bankroll 50 times your largest bet. $5 bet means you should have $250 just to start.

9. Have a stop loss limit - know when to quit when losing.

10. Control your emotions.

Currency Devaluation -Vegas Style. You exchange your money for chips or cheques as they are called in the following order:

$	1.00	Cheques
$	5.00	Cheques or nickles
$	25.00	Cheques or quarters
$	100.00	Cheques or one big one
$1000.00		Cheques or big dime

Money is macho - makes the male ego build. He likes to show off to the other players, female companions, public in general. Vegas will psyche you into wanting to lose, in fact players want to lose. You see many players just walk off leaving a winning hand or winning roll of the dice at the table. Many winning

45

keno tickets are never collected. To gain the mental-winning edge before gambling you must:

1. Know your game,
2. Have money management plan,
3. Have self control,
4. Have a game plan,
5. Gamble smart - don't drink and gamble.

"SHOW ME A HAPPY LOSER, AND I WILL SHOW YOU A SUCKER"

House advantages per game are:

Roulette	5.26%
Craps	1.41% pass-come bets up to 16% on prop bets
Baccarat	5.00% commission on bank bets
Blackjack (21)	2 to 10%
Slots-Video games	20%
Keno	25%
Poker	3 to 6% commission

We are now ready to give you a game plan for each game, so you can win and have fun in Las Vegas. Yes, you can win and a very definite YES, YES you can have fun.

CHAPTER 10

Baccarat

Baccarat (pronounced: Bah-Cah-rah) is considered the most fair game in gaming. Tourists just don't play the game because of the high stakes or bets required and often played. The minimum bet of $20 is considered by many to be more than they want to wager at one time. Most people bet small and this is why slots and video games are increasing in play. It is also why 50% of the revenue of a casino is from slots and video games. Look at any casino and you will see hundreds of machines.

Baccarat was imported to the U.S. from Cuba in 1959. Baccarat is considered a big money game, with wagers of $10,000 or more common in many Baccarat games. When first introduced to Las Vegas it was played with cash. This made it a high rollers game. Many times a million dollars would be on a table being bet or available to wager during the evening. Yes, most big games are played during the late evening hours. Baccarat brings out the ladies in evening gowns, men in tuxedos. The room or area of play is very elegant in furnishings and decor. Dealers dressed in tuxedos, pit boss in his finest attire and the finest of wines available to the players.

Baccarat is a game of three decisions.

1. Play Banker Side
2. Play Player Side
3. Play ties.

The probability of banker-hand winning is 45.9 %; player hand winning 44.6%; and ties 9.5%. Before we start the game we must get our terminology or language definitions.

DACCARAT - Big nine or card game looking for a point of 9.

BANKER - Designation of play - casino side. Player holding the shoe.

BURN CARDS - Cards discarded after each shuffle.

CARD VALUES - Values placed on each card. Face cards - 10 counts are zero.

BOOKMARK - Marker placed approximately 5/6 of way in shoe, alerts dealer to reshuffle.

CHEQUE - Terminology used for chips used in place of money.

COMMISSION - 5% charged on all wins by the bankers side of play.

DEALER - There are 3 assigned to each Baccarat table.

1 Caller (croupier) runs the game, directs the shoe, calls the game, directs pace of play, calls totals, announces the winner.

2-3 Dealers sit across from the caller -Collects bets, makes pay offs, keeps track of commission owed by each player.

DOESNOT DRAW - Players hand third card value action that stops play.

LAYOUT - Green floor of the playing field. Designates, banker play, player play, ties, number of players (most common 14), and boxes for commission owed by each player.

NATURAL - 8 or 9 point value of a hand that represents the highest hands you can receive in Baccarat. Play stops with a natural.

NINE - Highest winning score in Baccarat.

PLAYER - Player making the largest bet at the table is designated as the player side of the game. He handles the players cards.

TIES - Bacarrat hands equal value. They come up 9.5% of the time.

THIRD CARD
RULES - Rules of the Baccarat table that govern the draw of a third card.

SHOE - Device the dealer will use to deal the cards from. In Bacarrat it holds 8 decks.

WHEN GIVING - Giving player hand a third deck.

Baccarat is a random game, it makes no difference whether you choose Player-side or Banker-side to wager on. Baccarat is a game of luck, with a negative factor riding on every decision. We know the cards move in a pattern of ups and downs, with ties occuring 9.5% of the time. You can expect a player (player or banker) to win twice in a row about 25% of the time. You will see a player winning 3 times in a row 12% of the time and 5 times in a row only occurs about 3% of the time. Baccarat is a game of systems players. After much study and research we find no system works but, we will give you a system that will work if you let it work for you. See our Recommended Play at the end of this chapter.

How to play Baccarat requires no study, practice or tough decisions. The decisions are made for you by the way of rules. The dealers will direct you in play as they are trained in making decisions according to the rules. We are interested in playing only and leave the decisions to the dealers.

As you walk up to the table you will see numbers 1 thru 15, leaving out the No. 13, which leaves space for 14 players. Directly in front of you are two boxes for you to make your bet. They are marked player or banker, with bets for ties designated in a separate location. Three dealers are working the table.The caller who directs play on one side of the table and two dealers, each working one end of the table. Baccarat is similar to Blackjack as you are looking for a point of 9 as the winning number. Blackjack the winning number is 21. Values of cards are different from Blackjack as face cards value is zero, aces are one and all number cards as listed (6 equals 6, while 10 equals 0). The value of your hand is always the last digit of the number.

Samples:

3 and 4	equals 7	6 and 2	equals 8
10 and 5	equals 5	1 and queen	equals 1
4 and 5	equals 9	2 and ace	equals 3

Dealing the hand is done by a player designated as banker. The shoe is rotated counter-clockwise around the table to each player. When you have the shoe you are called the banker. The player only deals the cards, the casino is the real banker that collects and pays bets. Cards are dealt out face down, first to the player and then to the banker. Two cards are dealt to each. The dealer moves the players cards to the player who has the largest bet to be turned over. The dealer (caller) then turns the banks cards over. If a third card is required the caller will tell the player with the shoe to deal the player's hand a card. After this third card, rules prevail that dictate if the banker receives another or third card.

PLAYER THIRD CARD RULES

2 card value	Play.
0-5	Player must draw third card -unless bank has natural 8 - 9.
6-7	Player Hand must stand.
8-9	Natural Hand, both player and bank must stand.

BANK THIRD CARD RULES

2 card value	Play.
0-2	Bank must draw 3rd card unless player has natural.
3	Bank Hand draws if Player Hand draws anything except 8.
7	Bank draws if player draws 2 - 3 - 4 - 5 - 6 - 7.
5	Bank Hand draws if Player Hand draws 4 - 5 - 6.
6	Bank Hand draws if Player Hand draws 6 or 7.
7	Bank Hand must stand.
8 or 9	Natural Bank Hand both hands stand.

If either hand draws in 2 cards a natural (8 or 9) no one draws a third card. 9 beats an 8, and ties are a stand off.

The player is the first to act and will draw a third card if he does not have a total of 6 - 7 - 8 or 9.

When the player draws or stand, the bank draws to 0 - 1 and 2.

Pictures and tens count as zero. You are looking for a total of 9 and if you have a ten or face card and a 9 you have 19 or a natural 9 in Baccarat.

MINI-BACCARAT is just a scaled down version of the standard game and layout. Rules are the same and play of the game is similar. You have only one dealer who deals, calls, and pays-out and collects from all players. The minimum bet is usually $2. Mini-Baccarat was introduced for two reasons.

     1. Many people or players were scared of the high wagers.

     2. The lack of space in casinos.

RECOMMENDED PLAY:

     1. Always bet with the dealer on the initial deal after a shuffle. The Banker tends to win the first hand for some unknown reason.

     2. Every Casino will furnish you with a score card to list who won the last game. Player or Banker. Also keep track of the

5's as 5's are the most damaging card to a player's hand. The lesser number of fives in the remaining decks favor the player's hand. In 8 decks remember there are 32 fives, therefore if you have less than 10 fives in a shoe with approximately ½ of the cards remaining you should increase your bet on the player's side.

3. Money management. As we know a run of 3 wins only occurs 12% of the time. Bet in units of 1 - 2 - 3. On the first hand bet 1, if you win, add 1 cheque and bet 3 on the next game. If you win, reduce your bet by 5 back to one. This gives you Casino money to play with. Do this until you have 6 of the casino cheques, then increase your bet to 2 - 4 - 6. Bet 2 if you win, add 2 makes 6. If you win, pull off your winnings and start back at 2 cheques.

4. When you start a new bet line, bet opposite the last decision.

5. If you lose three games in a row, drop out 2 games and bet the opposite side of the last winning game.

6. Never try to win 4 games in a row, as they occur only 6% of the time. This is small odds to wager against.

To recap your play: Bet Bank on first play of a new Shoe.

Bet 1 cheque on players next game. If you win add 1 and bet 3 cheques second game. If you win reduce your bet by 5 cheques and return to bet 1. If you lose always return to one cheque bet.

Change to the banker on next game and bet 1 cheque. Repeat above game plan.

BACCARAT

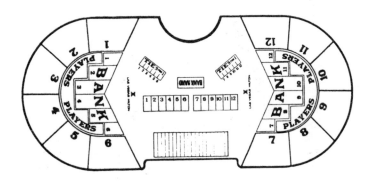

1. If Banker's hand or Player's hand has a total of 8 or 9 on their first two cards, this is a "natural". No additional cards are drawn, and a winner is determined immediately, unless a tie exists.

Pictures and tens do not count, Banker having 1-2-10 draws a third card — Banker must stand on 6 when Player does not draw a third card.

2. If neither hand has a "natural"

RULES

BANKER

When his first two cards total	Draws when player's third card is	Does NOT draw when player's third card is
3	1-2-3-4-5-6-7-9-10	8
4	2-3-4-5-6-7	1-8-9-10
5	4-5-6-7	1-2-3-8-9-10
6	6-7	1-2-3-4-5-8-9-10
7	STANDS	
8-9	NATURAL — STANDS	

PLAYER

HAVING	
1-2-3-4-5-10	DRAWS A CARD
6-7	STANDS
8-9	NATURAL — STANDS

MINI BACCARAT

CHAPTER 11

Blackjack (21)

Blackjack (21) is a card game that uses single or multi decks (2 - 4 - 6 - 8) of 52 cards per deck. The cards are shuffled at intervals set by the Casino. Cards are dealt from the dealer's left to right with the first player called first-base. There are 6 or 7 player positions per table and squares or circles are provided for each player to place their bet in. Also printed on the lay-out is table regulations on hitting soft 17, insurance and what a Blackjack (21) is paid. Before we start the game we must define the terms used.

ACE - A card that counts 1 or 11 in blackjack.

BLACKJACK - Any ace with any 10 that is received in first two cards. Face-cards have count of 10 in Blackjack.

BURN-A-CARD - Dealer must deposit one card from the top of the deck in the discard rack after each shuffle. Some casinos require more than one card be burned after each shuffle.

BUST - When the total count of all of your cards total more than 21.

CUT - After a shuffle the dealer offers the deck to a player to place a cut card in the approximate center of the deck. Player can cut the deck anywhere as he pleases. Cut thin and win is often said by players.

DEAL - Distribution of the cards by the dealer to the players.

DEALER - Person who deals, makes pay-offs and runs the game. He collects when you lose.

DOUBLE DOWN - A player doubles the size of his bet and receives one card. This is only done after the first two cards are dealt to the player.

DRAW - When a player receives additional cards.

FACE CARD - Any King, Queen or Jack. Count of all face cards is 10.

FIRST BASE - First player left of the dealer. He receives the first card from the dealer at the start of each game.

HIT - When a player wants an additional card - he asks for a hit (card).

HOLE CARD - The dealer's down card.

INSURANCE - A player bets when the dealer has an ace showing that his hole card is a 10 count, or the dealer has a Blackjack. Pays 2 to 1.

NATURAL - When a player has a 21 count in first 2 cards. Ace-10 or face card.

PAT - When player plays the original 2 cards dealt, he has a pat hand.

PUSH - When the player's cards count is the same as the dealers.

SHOE - Device the dealer will use to deal the cars from, when dealing more that 2 decks. Decks used in a shoe are 4 - 6 - 8.

SHUFFLE - To arrange the cards before they are dealt to the players.

SOFT HAND - A hand with an ace. Example Ace - 6 is either 7 or a soft 17. Ace can count 1 or 11.

SPLITTING - To divide two cards of identical count. Ace's, 9's, 8's. Any two cards of the same value can be split. Even 2 face cards.

STAND - To play with the cards you have - refuse additional cards.

THIRD BASE - Person that receives the last card before the dealer. Last player on the dealers right.

TOKE - What all dealers love to hear - a toke or tip for the dealer.

UP-CARD - Face up card to either dealer or player.

Now you are ready to play Blackjack (21). On each table will be a sign that gives the minimum bet for that table. Place your money on the lay-out (not in a circle) and ask for change - cheques. The dealer will issue you cheques per the denomination you request $1 - $5 - $25. Place your bet in the circle and the dealer is ready to deal the cards. He starts at first base, dealing one card to each player and one to the dealer. He repeats this again, but turning his second card face-up. Some casinos deal all players cards face-up. If your first 2 cards are Ace - 10 value, you have a Blackjack. It pays 3 to 2. Your bet is $10, you receive $15. Dealer will start at first base, asking each player if he wants additional cards. The object is getting 21 count without going over 21. If you go over 21 you bust, your hand is finished until next game. The dealer will go to each player asking if additional cards are needed. Then he turns over his down (hole) card, which he stands on 17 and hits anything under 17. Count determines the winners.

According to casino policy the dealer will repeat this deal and count game until the cards are used to a position the casino mandates a shuffle. To shuffle the dealer mixes the cards 3 or 4 times and strips them once. He then offers the deck to one player to cut. If no player cuts the cards the dealer is required to do so. He then burns one card - places one card in the discard rack. If more than one deck is used, some casinos require more than one burned card.

Blackjack can be played without a word spoken. To receive an additional card, signal the dealer by scraping your cards gently toward you. Repeat this as long as you need another card without going over 21. Possible plays you may have and what play you can use are:

DOUBLE DOWN - You have 9 - 10 - 11 (first 2 cards) dealer has an 8 or less as a up-card. Turn your cards over, double your bet and the dealer will give you one card. You can not bust (go over 21), therefore, you must see what the dealers card count is to find out if you win or lose.

SPLIT A PAIR - Player has a pair of Aces - 9's or 8's, dealer has a 7 for an up-card. You split the two cards into two hands. Double your bet and you receive one card only on aces or as many cards as you need on other pairs. Again, the final count with the dealer will determine if you win or lose.

BLACKJACK - Your original two cards are Ace - 10 or face card. Total count is 21, you have Blackjack. Pays 3 to 2.

SURRENDER - Very few casinos offer surrender. This is an option whereby you give up half of your bet and throw your cards in. Game is finished for you.

INSURANCE - Dealer has an ace up, will ask for insurance. You will be betting that the dealer has a Blackjack or a 10 count card down.

TOKES or TIPS - This is how the dealers make the majority of his pay for dealing the game. If you hit a Blackjack or have an unusually long run of winning hands, place a bet for the dealer. Place this bet directly in front of your bet on the circle. If you win the dealer wins. This makes the dealer want to assist you in winning more. Get his blessing and you will enjoy the game more.

You will hear about card counting. As a novice player, one who plays for fun and hopefully profit, forget card counting. On the next page I give you a map for playing every card, according to the dealers up-card. Learn this map and you will play with the best of players. This map has been devised after many years of playing and notes from the big boys. Card counting is for the professional player that hopes to earn a living playing Blackjack.

Money Management - Enough cannot be said about managing your money when gambling. Besides knowing the game, if you can manage your money properly, you will come out a winner.

67

When you come to Las Vegas divide your money into playing sessions. You come to Vegas for 3 days, have $600 to gamble with. Three days with $600 gives you $200 per day to gamble with. Take 2 sessions at the games, which gives you $100 each time you go to the tables. If it is your first time, get $50 in $1 and $50 in $5 cheques. Start small or with $1 until you learn the game, then increase your bet. The longer you play smart, the longer you keep your money.

Blackjack money management - As above, divide your money into gaming sessions. Plan on each session to last one to two hours. Never longer than 2 hours. You get drowsey, may drink too much, or just get bored. Also, if you start with $100 and your bankroll increases to $200, place the original $100 in your pocket never to be touched again this session. You get $300, place another $100 in your pocket, never to be touched this session. You have the picture, repeat this often and you will go home a winner.

Your Last bet was	you	you now bet
$1	win	3
$3	win	3
$3	lose	1

When you win, add one cheque to original bet, plus winnings. Revert back to one each time you lose. If you lose keep playing one until you win. If you lose 3 in a row, play one at a time until you win 3, then increase your bet to 3. Multiples of 3 until you reach 9, then go back to 1. I don't want you to lose your winnings, because if you have increased your bet to 9, that means you have been playing on house casino money. Keep it to play again.

RECOMMENDED PLAY - In the next few pages is a map for playing all hands of Blackjack according to your first 2 cards count and the dealers up-card.

ADDITIONAL RECOMMENDED PLAY IS:

DOUBLE DOWN - Only double down on your first 2 card count of 9 - 10 - 11 when the dealers up-card is 8 or less. Double down when you have an Ace duce (2), Ace three (3) when the dealers up-card is 3 thru 7.

SPLITTING PAIRS - Always split aces. You will receive one card on each ace, but your chances of winning is much greater than receiving a hit on the two aces.

BLACKJACK - When you receive a Blackjack (21) your first two cards and the dealers has an Ace up-card, call out EVEN-MONEY. You will be paid even money on your bet regardless of the dealers down-card. If you do not call out even-money, and the dealer has a Blackjack you have a push and do not get paid. This is the same as taking insurance..

SPLITTING PAIRS - Splitting Aces is always done. Other pairs that should be split on certain dealers up-card are: Tens (10 count or face cards) - Split only when dealers up-card is 4 - 5 - 6. This is different from the map, but it works.
Nine's (9) - Split only when dealers up-card is 4 - 5 - 6 - 7 - 8.
Eights (8) - Split only when dealers up-card is 4 - 5 - 6 -7.

Fives (5) - Never split fives. Double down on 5's if dealers up-card is 4 - 5 - 6 - 7. For further recommendations see the road-map on the next page.

MAP FOR BLACKJACK (21)

DEALER'S UP CARD

Players Hand	2	3	4	5	6	7	8	9	10	A C E
5-6-7-8	H	H	H	H	H	H	H	H	H	H
9-10-11	D	D	D	D	D	D	D	H	H	H
12	H	H	S	S	S	H	H	H	H	H
13-14-15-16	S	S	S	S	S	H	H	H	H	H
17-18-19-20	S	S	S	S	S	S	S	S	S	S
A2-A3-A4-A5	H	H	H	D	D	H	H	H	H	H
A-6	H	D	D	D	D	H	H	H	H	H
A-7	H	H	D	D	D	S	S	H	H	H
A-8	S	S	S	S	S	S	S	S	S	S
A-9	S	S	S	S	S	S	S	S	S	S
A-A	SP	SP	SP	SP	SP	SP	SP	SP	SP	SP
5-5	D	D	D	D	D	D	D	H	H	H
8-8	SP	SP	SP	SP	SP	SP	SP	H	H	H
9-9	SP	SP	SP	SP	SP	SP	SP	SP	SP	SP

H - Hit   D - Double Down   S - Stand   SP - Split

When you have 8-9-10-11-A8   Think, should I double.
When you have 12-13-14-15-16   Think, should I stand
When you have a pair Think, may I split, should I split.

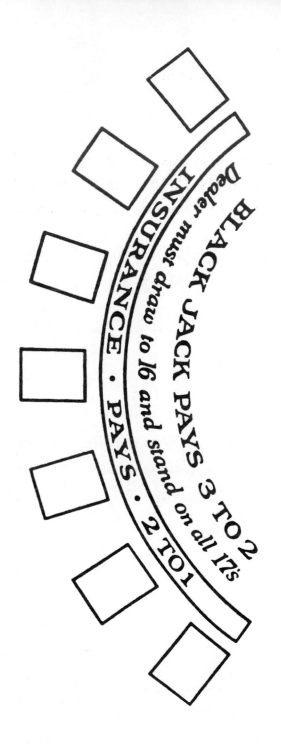

CHAPTER 12

CRAPS

Dice or Craps as they are called in Las Vegas is one of the most played games. You will see 10 to 16 men around a table looking down, hollering, screaming for seven or yo (11). They are engaged in the game of craps. Before I explain the game, we must learn the terms or language used on a Craps table.

BAR - To dissallow - casinos will bar either the 2 or 12 on the don't pass line. This is the house percentage.

BET - A wager between you and the casino.

BIG 6 OR BIG 8 - Bets located in the corner of the layout. They win when 6 or 8 is rolled and lose when 7 is rolled. They pay even money.

BOXMAN - The boss of the crap table. He sits down between the two dealers. He sits guarding the house chips of checks.

BUY BETS - Usually made on the 4 or 10, whereby, you receive true odds. A vig of commission of 5% is paid to receive true odds.

CHEQUES - Chips used in place of money on a Craps table, or gaming table.

COME BET - Delayed pass-line wager. You are making the bet while the shooter is trying to repeat a point-number.

COME-OUT ROLL - First roll of the dice by a player.

DEALER - Each table is assigned 4 dealers. Three working and one on break. Each dealer works 40 minutes on base and 20 minutes on stick.

DON'T PASS - A bet with the casino (opposite of the pass line).

DOUBLE ODDS - This wager is made after the shooter established a point. Most casinos allow you to take double your pass line bet for odds. You receive true odds on your pass-line odds bet. Each Craps table will have a sign to designate the amount of odds you can take, if not ask a dealer.

DROP BOX - Box attached to the Craps table where all cash is deposited. The box-man has control of the drop box.

EASY WAY - When you make a 4 - 6 - 8 - 10 without rolling a pair. Example: roll 8 by 5 and 3.

EYE IN THE SKY - Cameras that watch each game from the ceiling - out of sight.

FIELD BET - Designated area marked field bets -consist of 2 - 3 - 4 - 9 - 10 - 11 - 12. Many casinos pay double on 2's and triple on 12. You lose on 5 - 6 - 7 -8.

FULL ODDS - Maximum odds you can take on a bet that allows odds.

HARDWAY - Shooter rolls any 4 - 6 - 8 - 10 with a pair. Example: 10 made with 2 - 5's.

HORN BET - A proposition bet which consist of 2 -3 -11 - 12.

HORN HIGH BET - Same as horn bet except an extra chip is placed on one number. Example: 5 chips bet horn high 11. 2 - 3 - 12 have one chip - 11 has 2 chips.

LAY BET - A bet against a point number. Example: Nos 4 - 5 - 6 - 8 - 9 - 10 can have lay bets. You pay 5% vig or commission for the privilege of laying this bet.

LAY-OUT - The cloth used on all gaming tables. The designate the bets and odds allowed by the casino.

LIMIT - The maximum amount that can be bet. All tables have a sign posted giving the minimum and maximum amount of each bet.

NATURAL - 7 or 11 rolled on the come out roll. A winnner.

PARLAY - To bet your winnings and orginal bet again together.

PASS - A winning decision for the pass line bettors.

PASS LINE - Area designated for pass line bets. Bets with the shooter.

PIT - Area located behind the gaming tables.

PIT BOSS - Game supervisor responsible for all games in his area.

PLACE BET - A wager made on any or all of the point numbers without having to wait for the come-out roll. Casino does not pay true odds on place bets.

POINT - Number rolled on come-out roll other than 7 - 11 or 2 - 3 - 12. This number must be rolled again to win, before a 7 is rolled.

PRESS - To increase your bet when it wins.

PROPOSITION BETS - Bets located in the center of the layout. They are considered long shots. All have odds - see layout for odds given.

PUCK - Round Market used to designate a point made by the shooter.

SEVEN OUT - Shooter rolls a 7 after establishing a point number. You lose if you have your bet on the pass line, place bets, field bets, big 6 or 8.

SHOOTER - The person shooting or rolling the dice.

STICK - What the stickman uses to move the dice. Dealer using the stick is referred to as the stickman.

THREE WAY CRAPS - A prop bet on numbers 2 - 3 - 12.

TOKE - Tip for the dealers. They like to hear this word.

VIG - Commission (usually 5%) that you pay for the privilege of making a buy or lay bet.

WHIRL BET - A prop bet that includes the 2 - 3 - 7 -11 - 12.

YO-ELEVEN - Call made for 11 when rolled by the shooter.

There are 36 ways to roll the dice-points to be made.

(2) 1-1	(12) 6-6
(3) 2-1 1-2	(11) 6-5 5-6
(4) 2-2 3-1 1-3	(10) 5-5 6-4 4-6
(5) 2-3 3-2 4-1 1-4	(9) 4-5 5-4 6-3 3-6
(6) 3-3 4-2 2-4 1-5 5-1	(8) 4-4 5-3 3-5 6-2 2-6
(7) 4-3 3-4 5-2 2-5 6-1 1-6	

Now we are ready to go to the table. Look at the diagram on page 86 and see the positions of the box-man, dealers, stickmen and players. Now you drop your money (say $100) on the floor of the table. Dealer is not allowed to take money from your hand. He will exchange it for cheques to be used in making your bets. Listen to the stickman say "they are coming out". Make your bet by placing it on the pass line (House advantage is 1.4%). After a point is established you are allowed to make an odds bet -placed behind your pass line bet. Double odds means you can bet 2 times your pass line bet. Example: Your pass line bet of $5 allows you to place up-to $10 odds. You receive true odds on this bet, always place this bet (odds on pass line bets).

Come bet is exactly the same as a Pass Line Bet, after the shooter has established a point. It wins and loses the same as the Pass Line Bet. When you make a come bet, after the shooter rolls the dice, your bet is moved to the number rolled by the shooter. Your bet is placed in the number box according to the position you are playing at the table. If the shooter repeats the number you win, if he rolls a 7 you lose.

Odds given for pass line and come bets are:

(4 -10	2 to 1)	(5 -9	3 to 2)
(6 - 8	6 to 5)		

COME BET WITH ODDS - You can take odds on come bets same as pass line bets. you are paid true odds, just like pass line odds bet.

DON'T PASS LINE - The opposite of pass line bet -You are betting with the casino and against the shooter.

LAYING ODDS ON DON'T PASS LINE BET -Opposite of pass line odds. You are laying the same odds as the casino for the number rolled. Example: 5 is rolled, you lay 3 checks to win 2.

DON'T COME BET - Same as Don't Pass Line Bet. Laying Odds on Don't Come Bet - Same as laying odds on Don't Pass Line Bet.

PLACE BETS - A bet on any of the box numbers, 4 - 5 - 6 - 8 - 9 - 10.

You tell the dealer the number or numbers you want to bet on, the amount of the bet and he will place your bet on the double lines around the number you requested. You are betting this number will roll before 7. If a 7 rolls you lose.

Place bets are with odds which are:

	4 and 10	5 & 9	6 & 8
Odds	9 to 5	7 to 5	7 to 6
House %	6.7	4.0	1.5

You must bet in round figures as the percent of the bet. Example: On 6 and 8 you must lay 6 checks to receive 7. 4 - 10 you lay 5 to get 9 checks. 5 - 9 lay 5 checks to get 7. You can take these bets down at any time.

BUY BETS - Buy bets pay true odds and you can select any number. Any time the number rolls you win. If a 7 comes up you lose. To buy a bet you must pay a 5% vig or commission to the casino.

LAY BETS - Opposite of buy bets. You select a number and bet it doesn't roll before a 7 is rolled. Again you pay the Casino 5% Vig.

FIELD BETS - Designated area marked Field Bets with numbers of 2 - 3 - 4 - 9 - 10 - 11 - 12. most Casinos pay double on 2's and triple on 12's. This bet is for one roll of the dice. House advantage is 5.6% for a field bet.

BIG 6 AND 8 BETS - Located in the corner of the layout. You can bet that number will come up before a 7. This bet pays even money. This is a sucker bet.

PROPOSITION BETS - Located in the center of the layout table. The stickman is responsible for positioning these bets, telling the dealer the payout and taking them down when they lose.

Proposition Bets are:

(Hard 4	(2-2)	8 for 1)	(Any Crap	8 for 1)
(Hard 10	(5-5)	8 for 1)	(Any 7	5 for 1)
(Hard 6	(3-3)	10 for 1)	(Eleven (6-5)	16 for 1)
(Hard 8	(4-4)	10 for 1)	(Craps (2 or 12)	31 for 1)
			(Craps 3 (1-2)	16 for 1)

Please note that 8 for 1 is not the same as 8 to 1. "FOR" means you don't keep your original bet. "TO" means you keep your original bet plus winnings.

RECOMMENDED PLAY:

PASS LINE - To be in the flow of the game always place your pass line bet and take odds. Taking odds reduces the house advantage.

DON'T PASS LINE - DON'T COME LINE: These two bets are placed when you believe the shooter is going to lose. You are betting with the Casino. Take this bet only when shooters are not making their point.

FIELD: Notice on lay-out (Field 2 - 3 - 4 - 9 - 10 - 11 -12). Take this bet when a shooter throws the dice off the table. On the next roll of the dice, place a field bet. House advantage is 5.6%.

CORNER 6 or 8: Don't take these bets. These are sucker bets.

PLACE BETS: After being at a table for several rolls, you see that shooters are making points, place the following PLACE BETS. (Give this bet to the dealer, he will make it for you).

Shooter makes a 6 or 8 on come-out roll. Place 5 and 9. (odds are 7 to 5) Every time a 5 or 9 comes up you receive payment. If the shooter rolls a seven you lose. On come-out rolls, place bets are off (you do not lose or win).

PROPOSITION (PROP) BETS: All of the bets listed above are PROP BETS, located in the center of the lay-out. When you have a lucky streak going (winning) make a horn bet (2 - 3 - 11 - 12). If either number comes up you win the odds listed on the lay-out for that number. Horn bets are good when a shooter throws the dice off the table. The next roll place your bet on the horn bet. (Give this bet to the dealer - he will place it for you).

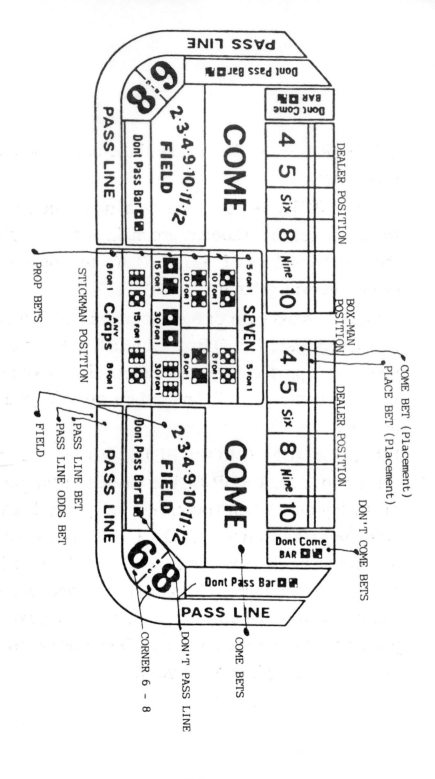

NOTE: Odds on Prop bets vary at each Casino.

CHAPTER 13

KENO

Keno the game everyone plays. Keno runners (girls dressed up cute) go to the many restaurants and bars in a Casino to get most of the bets made on Keno during a race. In every place you will see a big display board listing the numbers being drawn on a Keno race, people marking a Keno form, making a small but important Keno wager. The risk may be a dollar, and sometimes less than a dollar, but they are making a Keno wager. This is what makes Keno go, this is what makes Keno a winner, this is what makes Keno profitable for the casino.

Keno is the fore-runner of today's lotteries. Invented in China and brought to the U.S. by the Chinese, Keno is basically a numbers game. The Chinese used 120 characters or numbers. The American way has reduced it down to the 80 numbers we use today. Keno was one of the first games legalized in Nevada in 1931, but it has undergone many changes. First known as Race-Horse Keno, the name Keno has stuck and each game has become known as a race. Keno is simple.

Keno is not the place for serious money. Keno is convenient. You can win big money for a small wager if you are lucky. Note the word LUCKY, as we mean L U C K Y. No skill, no education, no nothing will help once you learn how to write the game on a score sheet. Nevada is the only state that has legalized Keno.

Keno is drawn by electronic equipment, noting on a electronic board all of the 20 numbers selected out of the 80 possible. The 80 numbers are divided into two groups which serve no purpose. On the electronic boards you will see the numbers drawn, the number of the race (game) and when the game is closed. All races must be collected before another race begins. In preparation for the game (race) you must mark casino issued tickets, using a black crayon supplied by the Casino. No pens or pencils are allowed. In marking your ticket you are guessing which numbers will appear on the display board. The casino selects 20 out of the possible 80. You can select up-to 15 numbers and combinations of these 15 numbers. Get 8 numbers you win $50,000 for a $2 bet. High odds, High stakes gaming, High odds against you and every player of Keno.

The size of your payoff is determined by the amount you have wagered, the total number of spots or numbers you have marked, and the total number of spots that you have marked correctly. The correct term for the numbers you mark in Keno is spots. On pages 94 - 96 you will see a Keno game sheet provided by a local Casino. It will show you if you select up-to 15 numbers and get 8 out of 8 you can win $50,000 for a $2 bet. Most experienced Keno players limit their tickets to no more than eight spots. The most common is four, six or eight numbers. Notice the pay-schedule is directly based on the amount you have bet. You can wager up-to 10 games at one time. Note the game ticket on page 94 and you will see it list the first race and the last race. In the upper right hand corner is the price per game. This is what you want to wager on each game.

Keno rules require that you wait until all games are over before you collect on your ticket, regardless of the number of games you hit. You must collect before the start of the 11th game as all tickets are collected after each game. If you wait, you lose. Even if you use a Keno runner, you are responsible for collecting a winning ticket before the start of the next race. Most casinos run a disclaimer on the ticket blanks, "We are not responsible for Keno runners tickets not collected before start of next game".

Once you have marked your ticket you must present this ticket to the many Keno writers in the Keno lounge or a Keno runner will do this for you. Experienced Keno players prefer to take their tickets to the Keno lounge to get it validated. If not validated, stamped, and written by the Keno writers you do not have a legal Keno ticket. Note - the Casino limits its liability for each race to $50,000 for all winning tickets for that race. Your ticket will carry a disclaimer reading "$50,000 limit to aggregate players each game or race". This means that the winnings of all players cannot be over $50,000 and each player will receive a pro-rated share of the $50,000. But, do not be afraid, not many races have a total pay-out of $50,000. You will get your total winnings in 99.9999% of the time.

The selection of the numbers is done by two systems of random selection of numbers approved by the Gaming Board of Nevada. The most popular system features a rotating cage called "squirrel cage", in which all ping-pong balls are mixed. The machine operator simply trips a lever to trap a ball and force it into a display tube called "rabbit ears". Each ear contains or traps 10 balls on which a number is marked. Then one of the 20 numbers is called for a Keno race. Once all 20 are trapped and the numbers called the race is over. The casinos keep accurate records of the numbers drawn to make sure a random draw is made each time. Also, the Gaming Commission will check balls and the system used to make sure that the balls or numbers selected at random or chance, not by pre-arranged methods.

The other system used is a blower system - using forced air to blow the ping pong balls into the rabbit ears. The Casinos believe the air-system has more eye appeal and creates more random-selection to the process.

STRAIGHT TICKET - You mark a determined amount of spots and they win according to the schedule on page 95. Example: You select 4 numbers and get all 4 numbers, you wager $2 - you will win $224.

PAGES

SPLIT TICKET - You mark 8 numbers. The casino calls it 2 ways of hitting 4 numbers or spots on each ticket. You wager on each set of numbers or each way - 4 numbers.

WAY TICKET - A grouping of numbers added together to form different ways to win a Keno race. Example: you mark 4 groups of 4 numbers or a total of 16 numbers. You circle the numbers, the ways you want a race to be marked. There are 20 ways to make a 6-spot ticket using six groups of two numbers. Check your Keno form at the Casino for their approved method of grouping or marking a ticket.

COMBINATION TICKET - A fancy way to mark a way ticket. Example: You have marked 3 groups of 4 -combination ticket markings are 3/4 ways - 3/8 ways and 1/12 way. Assume you wager $1 on each way - your total bet is $7.

The high odds of winning are what make the jackpots big. The high cost of running a Keno game (runners - equipment - casino space) forces the casino to make a high percentage of the take on each race. The average casino will run 200 Keno races per day. Average ticket play is $3. You can see the handle or average ticket price will create alot of expense just to write, pay, and keep records. The casino selects 20 numbers out of possible 80 which would mean 3 to 1 odds. The casino pays-off 2 to 1, not 3 to 1. They keep your original bet and pay 2 to 1 making it 3 for 1. Note on Keno rate sheet that 1 number pays $3 for a $1 wager.

Most casinos have special tickets or races for you to mark. You must check with the Keno lounge for this information.

RECOMMENDED PLAY:

MARK WAY TICKET -

- 2 groups of 4 numbers. You now have 1 way of 8, 6 ways of 4, 4 ways of 2 total ways played is 11. Wager 50^c on each or a total of $5.50. Numbers we suggest are

16-17-18-19   51-52-53-54

Use your birthday, age, street number. All 4 numbers grouped together are good. Watch the race board to see the what numbers have been coming up. Play next to them.

KENO RULES

We pay on the original ticket.
Please check your machine vended ticket for accuracy. All payoffs are made on the original copy. The original copy is designated as the copy presented by the customer each game.

$50,000.00 Limit to aggregate players.
The total payout to all participating players on a single keno game is limited to $50,000.00.

Winning tickets must be cashed immediately.
Federal regulations require that all winning tickets must be presented for payment immediately after each keno game and before the start of the next game.

Keno runners are provided for your convenience.
Since runners must transport tickets from outlying service areas to the keno counter for proper validation, mark your tickets early to avoid missing a game. However, we will not be responsible for the runner's failure to get tickets validated on the current game.

Games are played every few minutes.
You may play as many tickets as you wish on each game for any multiple of the rates listed in the pay charts.

FOR ADDED EXCITEMENT PLAY WAY TICKETS

4 Groups of 2

4 Way 2	
6 Way 4	
4 Way 6	
1 Way 8	
Cost $15.00	

$1.00 per way

Catch	Pay
1-1-0	
1-1-0-0	4.00
1-1-1-0	
2-0-0-0	10.00
2-1-0-0	15.00
2-1-1-0	20.00
2-1-1-1	28.00
2-2-0-0	49.00
2-2-1-0	148.00
2-2-1-1	249.00
2-2-2-0	417.00
2-2-2-1	1,947.00
2-2-2-2	3,608.00
	31,640.00

$1.00 Rate

10 Groups of 3
45 way 6
$.25 per way
Cost: $11.25

20 Groups of 4
190 way 8
$.10 per way
Cost: $19.00

WAY TICKETS CAN BE PLAYED AT REDUCED RATES

HOW TO PLAY KENO

Mark your ticket.
Obtain a crayon and blank ticket from one of the many convenient locations in the club. Mark the ticket with at least one or as many as 15 of your favorite numbers. Use an "X" to cover the numbers and write the amount of your wager in the space provided. Consult the pay charts in this pamphlet for ticket prices and their payouts.

Place your bet.
Give the ticket, along with your wager, to one of our keno writers. A machine copy of your ticket showing the number of the game you are playing will be returned to you. Your ticket is good for that game only. **Please check your copy for accuracy.**

Check your ticket.
The numbered squares on your ticket correspond to the eighty numbered balls in the bowl. Each game, twenty balls are drawn at random and will appear as lighted numbers on keno boards located throughout the casino and in other services areas. Compare your ticket to the numbers that appear and consult the pay charts in this pamphlet to determine your payoff. If you have a winning ticket, present it to any keno writer for payment before the start of the next game. If you are in doubt or have any questions, any of our keno personnel are available to provide additional information.

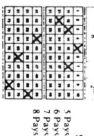

	$2.00 Rate
5 Pays	18.00
6 Pays	160.00
7 Pays	2,960.00
8 Pays	50,000.00

$1.00 RATE

SELECT 1 NUMBER

Winning Numbers	$1.00 Ticket Pays	$2.00 Ticket Pays	$7.50 Ticket Pays
1	3.00	6.00	22.50

SELECT 2 NUMBERS

Winning Numbers	$1.00 Ticket Pays	$2.00 Ticket Pays	$7.50 Ticket Pays
2	12.00	24.00	90.00

SELECT 3 NUMBERS

Winning Numbers	$1.00 Ticket Pays	$2.00 Ticket Pays	$7.50 Ticket Pays
2	1.00	2.00	7.50
3	42.00	84.00	315.00

SELECT 4 NUMBERS

Winning Numbers	$1.00 Ticket Pays	$2.00 Ticket Pays	$7.50 Ticket Pays
2	1.00	2.00	7.50
3	4.00	8.00	30.00
4	112.00	224.00	840.00

SELECT 5 NUMBERS

Winning Numbers	$1.00 Ticket Pays	$2.00 Ticket Pays	$7.50 Ticket Pays
3	1.00	2.00	7.50
4	14.00	28.00	105.00
5	720.00	1,440.00	5,400.00

SELECT 6 NUMBERS

Winning Numbers	$1.00 Ticket Pays	$2.00 Ticket Pays	$7.50 Ticket Pays
3	1.00	2.00	7.50
4	4.00	8.00	30.00
5	88.00	176.00	660.00
6	1,480.00	2,960.00	11,100.00

SELECT 7 NUMBERS

Winning Numbers	$1.00 Ticket Pays	$2.00 Ticket Pays	$7.50 Ticket Pays
4	2.00	4.00	15.00
5	20.00	40.00	150.00
6	380.00	760.00	2,850.00
7	8,000.00	16,000.00	50,000.00

SELECT 8 NUMBERS

Winning Numbers	$1.00 Ticket Pays	$2.00 Ticket Pays	$7.50 Ticket Pays
5	9.00	18.00	67.50
6	80.00	160.00	600.00
7	1,480.00	2,960.00	11,100.00
8	8,000.00	16,000.00	50,000.00

SELECT 9 NUMBERS

Winning Numbers	$1.00 Ticket Pays	$2.00 Ticket Pays	$7.50 Ticket Pays
5	4.00	8.00	30.00
6	44.00	88.00	330.00
7	300.00	600.00	2,250.00
8	4,000.00	8,000.00	30,000.00
9	25,000.00	50,000.00	50,000.00

SELECT 10 NUMBERS

Winning Numbers	$1.00 Ticket Pays	$2.00 Ticket Pays	$7.50 Ticket Pays
5	2.00	4.00	15.00
6	20.00	40.00	150.00
7	136.00	272.00	1,020.00
8	960.00	1,920.00	7,200.00
9	4,000.00	8,000.00	30,000.00
10	25,000.00	50,000.00	50,000.00

SELECT 11 NUMBERS

Winning Numbers	$1.00 Ticket Pays	$2.00 Ticket Pays	$7.50 Ticket Pays
5	1.00	2.00	7.50
6	8.00	16.00	60.00
7	72.00	144.00	540.00
8	360.00	720.00	2,700.00
9	1,800.00	3,600.00	13,500.00
10	12,000.00	24,000.00	50,000.00
11	28,000.00	50,000.00	50,000.00

SELECT 12 NUMBERS

Winning Numbers	$1.00 Ticket Pays	$2.00 Ticket Pays	$7.50 Ticket Pays
6	5.00	10.00	37.50
7	32.00	64.00	240.00
8	240.00	480.00	1,800.00
9	600.00	1,200.00	4,500.00
10	1,480.00	2,960.00	11,100.00
11	12,000.00	24,000.00	50,000.00
12	24,000.00	50,000.00	50,000.00

SELECT 13 NUMBERS

Winning Numbers	$1.00 Ticket Pays	$2.00 Ticket Pays	$7.50 Ticket Pays
6	1.00	2.00	7.50
7	16.00	32.00	120.00
8	80.00	160.00	600.00
9	720.00	1,440.00	5,400.00
10	1,480.00	2,960.00	11,100.00
11	8,000.00	16,000.00	50,000.00
12	16,000.00	32,000.00	50,000.00
13	25,000.00	50,000.00	50,000.00

SELECT 14 NUMBERS

Winning Numbers	$1.00 Ticket Pays	$2.00 Ticket Pays	$7.50 Ticket Pays
6	1.00	2.00	7.50
7	10.00	20.00	75.00
8	80.00	160.00	600.00
9	320.00	640.00	2,400.00
10	1,000.00	2,000.00	7,500.00
11	3,200.00	6,400.00	24,000.00
12	16,000.00	32,000.00	50,000.00
13	25,000.00	50,000.00	50,000.00
14	40,000.00	50,000.00	50,000.00

SELECT 15 NUMBERS

Winning Numbers	$1.00 Ticket Pays	$2.00 Ticket Pays	$7.50 Ticket Pays
7	8.00	16.00	60.00
8	28.00	56.00	210.00
9	132.00	264.00	990.00
10	300.00	600.00	2,250.00
11	2,600.00	5,200.00	19,500.00
12	8,000.00	16,000.00	50,000.00
13	16,000.00	32,000.00	50,000.00
14	32,000.00	50,000.00	50,000.00
15	40,000.00	50,000.00	50,000.00

MULTI-RACE KENO

MARK PRICE HERE

$50,000.00 LIMIT TO AGGREGATE PLAYERS EACH GAME

WE PAY ON TICKET SUBMITTED BY CUSTOMER BEFORE EACH GAME

1	2	3	4	5	6	7	8	9	10
11	12	13	14	15	16	17	18	19	20
21	22	23	24	25	26	27	28	29	30
31	32	33	34	35	36	37	38	39	40

WINNING TICKET MUST BE CASHED BEFORE START OF NEXT KENO GAME

41	42	43	44	45	46	47	48	49	50
51	52	53	54	55	56	57	58	59	60
61	62	63	64	65	66	67	68	69	70
71	72	73	74	75	76	77	78	79	80

KENO RUNNERS ARE AVAILABLE FOR YOUR CONVENIENCE
WE ARE NOT RESPONSIBLE IF TICKETS ARE TOO LATE FOR CURRENT GAME

CHAPTER 14

POKER

We have heard all of our life about playing Poker. Las Vegas Style Poker is usually limited to two types of poker. Seven Card Stud and Texas Holdem. Since we are describing Las Vegas style games we will limit our discussion to these two games. Now to our terminology of the games.

ADVERTISE - To bluff, to mislead your opponents on your method of play.

ALL-IN - To bet all the money you have in front of you.

ANTE - A bet made by everyone playing before the cards are dealt.

BUMP-RAISE - To increase the bet previously made by another bettor.

BURN - To discard the top card from a deck before cards are dealt to the players.

BUY-IN - The cheques you buy when entering a game.

BY-ME - An expression of saying to pass.

CHEQUE - Form of money used in betting instead of green backs.

CHECK - To pass or to bet nothing.

CUT - To separate the cards in the middle and place bottom half on top.

DOWN CARDS - The cards dealt to you face down.

NICKELS - A casino chip with the value of $5.

POT - The area on the table where all bets are place.

RAKE - Percentage the casino charges for dealing the game.

SHILL - A person in the employment of the casino, used to start a game. They are used to fill a table, start a game or entice you to play.

SHOWDOWN - Decision time at the end of betting to find the winner. All players must show their cards at this time to find the winner.

TOKE - A tip, what the dealer likes to hear.

RANKING OF POKER HANDS:

ROYAL FLUSH - Ace, King, Queen, Jack, Ten all of the same suit. Best hand in Poker. There are 4 of these hands in each deck.

STRAIGHT FLUSH - Any 5 cards in sequence of the same suite. The higher the ranking or number the higher the hand. Example: 5 - 6 - 7 - 8 - 9 spades.

FOUR OF A KIND - Any 4 cards of the same denomination. Example: 4 Kings.

FULL HOUSE - Three (3) cards of the same denomination, and two (2) cards of the same denomination to make your five cards. The hand with the highest 3 cards, in a full house wins. Example: 3 Kings - 2 Queens.

FLUSH - All 5 cards of the same suit, (Hearts, Diamonds, Clubs or Spades). These cards are not in sequence and the higher the cards denomination the higher the ranking of the flush.

STRAIGHT - All five cards in sequence, but not of the same suit. The highest card determines the winning straight, if more than one straight appears.

THREE OF A KIND - Three cards of the same value. Example: 3 Kings.

TWO PAIR - Two sets of two cards of the same value. Example: 2 Kings and 2 Queens. Higher the pairs the higher the hand is in value.

ONE PAIR - Two cards of the same value. Higher the value of the cards the higher value of the hand. Example: 2 Jacks.

THINGS TO KNOW IN A POKER GAME:

1. Know how much money is in the pot.

2. Know how many cards have been discarded that can help your hand. Memory is a great asset in playing poker.

3. Know you cannot play every hand out and win.

4. Know the other players. In Las Vegas you have Poker Players who play nothing else but Poker. They know the game, cards, money in pot, and soon will know your method of play. Watch a game for 30 minutes before you start to play.

5. Know your bankroll. Don't over bet your bankroll. Don't over bet your hand. Every game of Poker has its ups and downs, be able to stand all events of a game.

6. Know the casino will rake or take 5 to 10% of each hand for their expense, profit and etc.. Realize that in a winning hand a lot of this money is

yours, not profit or winnings.

7. Know when to quit. If you get ahead 2 times your original investment, then it is time to rest. If you lose 5 hands in a row, it is time to rest. Know when to rest after a winning or a losing session.

8. Know long poker sessions will make you drowsey. Plan on playing no longer than 2 hours before you rest. Leave the game for awhile.

After studying the terminology of the game and re-reading the things to know is a poker game, it is time to play. We will discuss each of the two games separate and give you suggestions of play.

7 CARD STUD - The dealer, gives each player two cards face down, and then one card face up. The lowest card is required to make the first bet to try to keep as many players in the game as possible. Then an additional card is dealt up, bet is made by the highest hand face-up. This is repeated until you have 4 cards dealt face-up and betting is done on the deal of each card. Betting started by the highest up-cards after the first up-card. The seventh (7) card is dealt down to the players still playing. You will find many

players will throw their cards in or quit playing after seeing 1 - 2 or 3 of the up-cards of other players. Final betting is done with 4 up-cards and 3 down-cards of all players. Show-down time is made after no more than 3 raises are made. The highest hand wins. Note: The casino takes its cut or percentage out of the pot and deposits it in a drop-box. The only time a bet is required is the first up-card, but to stay in to receive more cards you must place in the pot the amounts of any bets made on any of the other 3 cards dealt. To see the show-down you must cover any bets made on the last or seventh card. Show-down will determine the winner.

The odds on obtaining a hand from the first 3 cards dealt are:

Any pair	5 to 1
Any 3 of a Kind	424 to 1
3 Card Straight	5 to 1
3 Card Flush	24 to 1
3 Card Straight Flush	85 to 1

The odds for making a hand from the 3 cards dealt are even higher. Odds against making a full house out of two pair is 4 to 1. This gives you an idea of the odds against you in making a hand from the first 3 cards.

RECOMMENDED PLAY:

When you start with bad cards (first 3 cards), you have no place to go but lose. You stay with 3 cards, the 4th card helps you and this gives you a hand that comes in second. Seconds don't pay. How to play the first 3 cards are the most important play of a poker hand.

THREE OF A KIND - Odds are great against you getting this hand. Play it out, covering all bets. Make no raises until the 6th card. You want the pot to build, as you have a winning hand in most games.

PAIR ACES - KINGS - A pair of Aces or Kings are a good starting point. Watch the table if another of your cards is showing, this reduces the chances of you bettering your hand. After the 5th card if betting is heavy and you have not increased the value of your hand, throw it in.

PAIR QUEENS - JACKS - Open pair of Queens or Jacks (one is showing) reduces the value of your hand. Again if heavy betting appears after the 5th card and you have not increased the value of your hand, throw it in.

103

THREE CARDS STRAIGHT FLUSH - Good hand to start with. Bet or increase the bet the first round. With this hand you have several ways to help it. After the 5th card you have not increased its value, then throw it in.

3 CARDS TO FLUSH - With this hand you should complete a flush 1 out of 6 hands. Hold it until after the 5th card is dealt. If you have not received another card to your flush, throw it in.

3 HIGH CARDS, SMALL PAIR, 3 CARD TO STRAIGHT - After the 4th card you have not increased their value, throw your hand in. You must have cards to work with to be a winner. Wait until the next hand, don't bet all of your bankroll on a losing hand.

TEXAS HOLD'M:

Texas Hold'm is played on a table to as many as 11 players. The dealer shuffles and cuts the cards. He indicates the dealer from one of the players. He deals clock-wise to each player 2 face-down cards. The player next to the dealer is required to place a blind bet into the pot. There is a round of betting after the first two cards are dealt. The dealer burns a card from the deck and deals 3 cards face up in the center of the table - this is called the flop. Another round of betting is done. The dealer then burns another card and deals another card face-up. Another round of betting is made. The 7th and final card is dealt face-up to be used by all players. Your hand is now to be completed by the 2 cards you have down and the 5 up-cards or community cards in the center of the table. Final round of betting is done and showdown occurs. The highest hand wins, using the 2 down cards and 5 up-cards. This game is very similar to 7 Card Stud, except the 5 up-cards are used by all players in determining the winning hand.

RECOMMENDED PLAY FROM FIRST 2 CARDS:

Pair Aces - Hold and bet from first round. Best hand you can start with.

Pair Kings - Hold and bet from first round. Second best hand to start with.

Pair Queens or Jacks - Hold and cover all bets until the 5th card, if you have not increased the value of your hand, throw it in.

Two High Value Cards (King-Queen) - Hold an cover all bets until 4th card, if you have not increased the value of your hand, throw it in.

Two High Value Cards Suited - (King-Queen Spades) - Hold until after the 4th card and if you have not increased the value of your hand, throw it in.

Small Pair - (Pair of Eights) - Hold until 4th card, if you have not increased its value, throw it in.

After the flop (3 cards dealt up) if you have not received a hand that will beat a pair of Aces throw your hand in. Pair of Aces or better win most pots. Do not come to Las Vegas to learn to play poker in a short period of time. Poker is a game of skill, not chance and Vegas has many players that are very skilled. If you must play, limit your bankroll to a small portion of your entire bankroll for these games.

LAS VEGAS GUIDE TO POKER ROOMS

Bally Grand	7 card stud	Hold'm	high stakes
Barbary Coast	7 card stud		Low stakes
Ceasars Palace	7 card stud	Hold'm	Med stakes
Circus Circus	7 card stud	Hold'm Hi-Low Split	
			Low stakes
Desert Inn	7 card stud	Hold'm	Low stakes
Dunes	7 card stud		Hi-Low Splits
			Med stakes
El Rancho	7 card stud	Hold'm	Low stakes
Four Queens	7 card stud	Hold'm	Low stakes
Fremont	7 card hi-lo split	5 cards lo-ball	
			Low stakes
Frontier	7 card stud	Hold'm	no limit
Gold Coast	7 card stud	Hold'm	Low stakes
Gold Nugget	7 card stud	Hold'm Omaha no limit	
Hacienda	7 card stud	Hold'm	Low stakes
Holiday Inn	7 card stud	Hold'm	Low stakes
Imperial Palace	7 card stud	Hold'm Omaha hi-lo	
			Low stakes
Landmark	7 card stud	Hold'm Omaha hi-lo	
			Low stakes
Las Vegas Club	7 card stud	Hold',m	Low stakes
Las Vegas Hilton	7 card stud	Hold'm	Hi-Low
	7 card lo ball	Omaha	High stakes
Marina	7 card stud	Hold'm	Low stakes
Maxim	7 card stud	Hold'm	Hi-Low
			Low stakes
Mint	7 card stud	Hold'm	Low stakes
Nevada Palace	7 card stud	Hold'm	Hi-Low
			Low stakes
Palace Station	7 card stud	Hold'm	Low stakes

107

LAS VEGAS GUIDE TO POKER ROOMS ctd.

Poker Palace		Hold'm dealers choice
		Low stakes
Riviera	7 card stud	Hold'm Hi-Low
		Low stakes
Sahara	7 card stud	Hi-Low pan
		Low stakes
Showboat	7 card stud	Hold'm Low stakes
Silver Nugget	7 card stud	Hold'm Low stakes
Silver Slipper	7 card stud	Hold'm dealers choice
		Low stakes
Stardust	7 card stud	Hold'm Omaha Razz
		High stakes
Sundance	7 card stud	Hold'm Low stakes
Tropicana	7 card stud	Hold'm Low stakes
Union Plaza	7 card stud	Hold'm Omaha Pan
		Low stakes

CHAPTER 15

ROULETTE

Roulette, as played in Las Vegas has 36 numbers plus zero and double zero making a total of 38 numbers you can play. The odds are figured on 36 numbers giving the house an edge of 5.25%. You can find Roulette wheels with only one zero, but very few in the United States. One zero is used in most European casinos, but two zeros are most common in Las Vegas.

Before we get into the game we need our terminology used in the game.

BANK - Each table has its own cheques for case of play by the player and ease of paying each player. Cheques used in the game are for that table only. The bank is the location on the Roulette table the cheques are kept.

BUY-IN - Amount of cheques you purchase before starting play on a Roulette table. You must purchase cheques as cash or other casino cheques are not used in play at a Roulette table.

CHEQUES - Name for the chips you use on a Roulette table to place your bet.

CORNER BET - Four numbered roulette bet that pays 8 to 1.

DEALER - The person who runs the game at the Roulette table.

DROP BOX - Box where the dealer deposits all cash that he received for cheques from the players. The dealer does not use cash.

DOUBLE STREET BET - A six number bet that pays 5 to 1. Also referred to as a double line bet. (see diagram on page 116).

HOUSE ADVANTAGE - The percentage the house receives in figuring the odds for each bet. Roulette advantage is 5.25%.

LIMIT - The maximum amount that you can bet -table limits are posted on each Roulette table. If not, ask the dealer the limits.

PARLAY - To bet your original bet plus any winnings you have on the next roll of the roulette ball.

SPLIT BET - A two number bet that pays 17 to 1. Placed between two numbers on the layout. Either number may be a winner.

STRAIGHT UP BET - A single number roulette bet that pays 35 to 1.

STREET BET - A roulette bet that pays 11 to 1.

Placed on one single line of 3 numbers. Also referred to as a three number bet.

TOKE - What the dealer likes to hear. Tip or toke bet for the dealer.

Now we are ready to play the game. Say you want to start with $100 in cheques, with a value of $1 each. Tell the dealer you want $100 worth of $1 cheques. Give him your money or casino chips and he will give you 5 stacks of one color cheques (20 per stack). Only you have this color of cheques to play with on the Roulette table. Usually each Roulette table has 8 (eight) colors of cheques to accommodate 8 players. Each player may have a different value on his cheques. The dealer will note this by placing one of each color on the rim of the wheel with the value of the cheques posted on the color. Each table has a minimum and most players play the minimum, therefore, the dealer does not post the color and value.

Look at the layout on page 116, you will notice 36 numbers, either red or black. Eighteen are red and eighteen are black. The two zero numbers are green. You can bet on all 38 numbers, but the odds are figured only on 36. The dealer spins the ball counter to the movement of the wheel. I don't know of any roulette dealer that can control the ball enough to tell you where it is going to land. You can now place your bet or bets as follows:

STRAIGHT UP - One number bet that pays 35 to 1.

STREET - End of the line of 3 numbers that pays 11 to 1.

DOUBLE STREET - Also called double line bet. End of the line between 2 rows of numbers or 6 numbers that pays 5 to 1.

ODD OR EVEN - An even bet on which the ball will land, odd number or even number. Zeros are not included in this bet. The casino receives this advantage.

RED OR BLACK - An even bet on which color the ball will land. Again the zeros are not included. Pays even money.

1 thru 18 - 19 thru 36. An even bet on the top half or bottom half of layout. Located on player side of the layout. Pays even money. Again the zeros are not included - casino advantage.

1st column - 2nd column - 3rd column - Referred to as a Column bet. Located at bottom of layout away from the dealer. Pays 2 to 1.

SPLIT BET - A bet placed between two numbers. Pays 17 to 1.

CORNER BET - Bet placed on the corner of 4 numbers. You win if the ball lands on either number. Pays 8 to 1.

TOP LINE BET - Referred to as a 5 number bet. Located on the top line covering the numbers 1 - 2 - 3 - 0 - 00. Pays 6 to 1.

COURTESY BET - Placed on line between 2nd and 3rd dozen numbers. (see layout). Covers zero and double zero. Same as a split bet. Pays 17 to 1. You can make this bet between the two numbers 0 - 00.

RECOMMENDED PLAY FOR ROULETTE:

Please refer to the layout for placement of each bet on page 118 .

TOP LINE BET - Do not bet, sucker bet.

STREET BET - Play with winnings only. Play 3 different street bets when betting on this action or type of bet.

COURTESY LINE BET - Do not bet.

DOUBLE LINE BET (double street) - Play only with winnings. Play 2 Double line bets. This covers 12 numbers (2 bets of 6 numbers each).

DOZENS BET - Play 2nd and 3rd dozens with 1 cheque each, also play corner bet of 7 - 8 - 10 - 11 with 1 cheque. If you win dozen bet you break even, if you win corner bet you win 5 cheques. Casino advantage is reduced on this type of betting.

CORNER BET - See above play on dozen bet and corner bet.

COLUMN BET - Not recommended.

STRAIGHT UP BET - Divide all numbers on wheel into 5 columns. Example shown on page 115. Bet one cheque on each of the numbers in the column you have selected to wager on. Watch the spin of the wheel and wager on the next spin in the same column that the number is in that the ball falls on. Note these numbers split the wheel into 5 sections. All numbers are in rotation. The ball tends to fall into the same section 3 to 4 times before moving to the next column.

SPLIT BET - Play in place of corner bet when wagering on dozens bet. Play 3 splits when using this method.

BASKET BET - Not recommended.

ROULETTE

RECOMMENDED PLAY - Straight-up-bet. Division of the wheel into columns and placing a bet on each of the number in the columns. Note the location of the columns and numbers on the wheel below. Follow the flow of the game and play in the column the last fall of the ball is in.

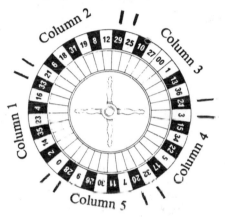

Clm 1	Clm 2	Clm 3	Clm 4	Clm 5
0	21	25	3	20
2	6	10	15	7
14	18	27	34	11
35	31	00	22	30
23	19	1	5	26
4	8	13	17	9
16	12	36	32	28
33	29	24		

Place one cheque on each number in the column you are paying. If you win you recieve 35 cheques. If you lose, you lose 7 or 8 cheques. Play small until you get the routine of the fall of the ball in the wheel. When you are winning is the time to increase your bets.

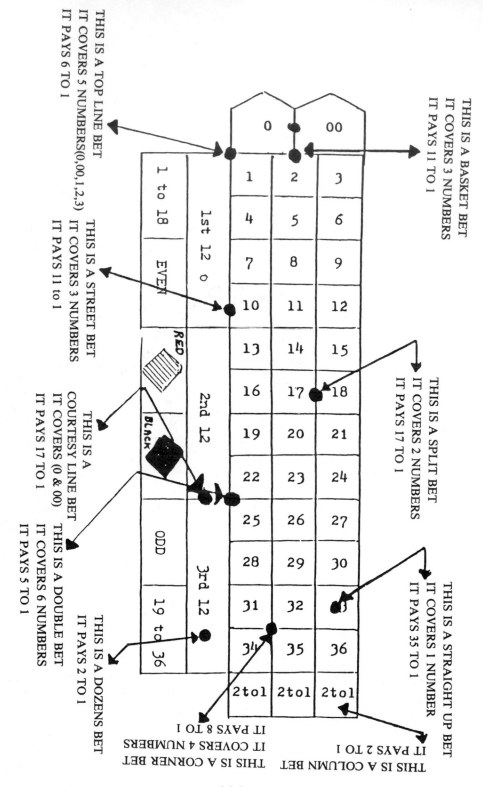

THIS IS A TOP LINE BET
IT COVERS 5 NUMBERS(0,00,1,2,3)
IT PAYS 6 TO 1

THIS IS A BASKET BET
IT COVERS 3 NUMBERS
IT PAYS 11 TO 1

THIS IS A STREET BET
IT COVERS 3 NUMBERS
IT PAYS 11 to 1

THIS IS A SPLIT BET
IT COVERS 2 NUMBERS
IT PAYS 17 TO 1

THIS IS A
COURTESY LINE BET
IT COVERS (0 & 00)
IT PAYS 17 TO 1

THIS IS A STRAIGHT UP BET
IT COVERS 1 NUMBER
IT PAYS 35 TO 1

THIS IS A DOUBLE BET
IT COVERS 6 NUMBERS
IT PAYS 5 TO 1

THIS IS A DOZENS BET
IT PAYS 2 TO 1

THIS IS A CORNER BET
IT COVERS 4 NUMBERS
IT PAYS 8 TO 1

THIS IS A COLUMN BET
IT PAYS 2 TO 1

116

CHAPTER 16

VIDEO POKER MACHINES

S lot machines are set at a pre-determined pay-off and you merely pull the handle or push a button to play. There are getting to be more and more slot machines in carousals that are progressive and give out larger pay-offs. Listed above these carousals is a total board listing the pay-offs as of the time you are ready to play. Look around the casino and find the largest pay-off carousal in terms of amount played (25ᶜ or 50ᶜor $1 or $5 and yes even 5ᶜ). In terms of pay-back these machines offer the best return for the money you want to invest or play. Find a slot machine that is played or in position to be played a lot and this is a machine that will give you a return quicker than machines never played. Slots are machines that make a lot of money for the casinos, therefore, you need to look at the machines to:

    1. Always start playing a machine that has been played last with the maximum amount of coins allowed.

    2. Look for coin wrappers around a machine.

If you find a lot of wrappers and no-one winning, you have a machine that should give a quick pay-out.

3. Look for a machine that people walk up, put maximum coins in several times and walk away.

4. Never put more than 3 turns at the machine without a winner. Always put in the maximum amount of coins the machine allows. After 5 turns at the machine if you are not a winner, at least even, move to another machine.

Remember the boy from Arkansas that was playing a $1 machine after his father played it and hit the big jackpot. He hit if for $1,060,000. Millionaire for a short time. Above this machine is a camera that records all winners. He was recorded as the player that hit the jackpot, under age he could not receive the money. Make sure you have two identifications with you. Drivers license and one other. No Casino will make a pay-out over $1,000 without you having proper identification.

Video Poker Machines resemble a slot machine in size, looks and arrangement in the Casino. You will find Twenty-one (21) machines, Keno machines, Horse-race machines, and several varities of Video Poker machines. We are going to expand on the

Video Poker machine. Regular Video Poker machines can be found dealing 52 cards, with jokers (wild - goes anything), dueces wild, dueces and jokers wild, in carousals (wired together to give a large pay-out - usually 8 to 12 machines). Our examples will be the regular Video Poker machine with 52 cards shuffled and dealt according to the percentage set in the machine.

Before we start with the play of the machines we need our terminology.

CREDIT MACHINE - Machine that issues points instead of coins after each win.

CASH-OUT BUTTON - Button used to receive your coins from a credit machine.

DEAL BUTTON - Button that starts the play of a machine.

DRAW BUTTON - Button that issues additional cards after initial 5 cards are dealt.

CANCEL BUTTON - Button that cancels your discards when an error is made.

HOLD BUTTON - Some machines have hold buttons for the cards you want to hold from the original 5 cards drawn.

STAND BUTTON - When you receive a pat or winning hand in the original 5 cards, you press the stand button to receive your winnings.

DISCARD BUTTON - Buttons you press to discard or do away with cards from the original 5 cards to allow additional card to be received.

TYPE OF WINNING HANDS YOU MAY RECEIVE ARE:

ROYAL FLUSH - Best hand you can receive. 5 cards of the same suit that include the Ace, King, Queen, Jack and Ten.

STRAIGHT FLUSH - Any 5 cards of the same suit in sequence.

Example: 8 - 9 - 10 - Jack - Queen of Hearts.

FOUR OF A KIND - Four 4 cards of the same value.

Example: 4 Kings.

FULL HOUSE - Three cards of the same value and 2 cards of the same value.

Example: 3 Queens and 2 six's.

FLUSH - Five cards of the same suit, not in the same sequence.

Example: All hearts of 1 - 5 - 9 - 10 - Jack -Ace.

STRAIGHT - Five cards in sequence but of different suits.

THREE OF A KIND - Three cards of the same value

- matching cards.

Example: 3 Queens, 1 - 9, 1 - 10.

TWO PAIR - Two sets of matching value cards. The 5th card can be anything.

Example: 2 Queens, 2 six's, and an Ace.

HIGHER PAIR - Note most machines return your original bet with Jacks or higher pair. A higher pair is either Jacks, Queens, Kings or Aces.

Types of pay-offs you may receive - The most common pay-off scale in Las Vegas will be as follows:

Hand	1 Coin	2 Coin	3 Coin	4 Coin	5 Coin
Royal Flush	250	500	750	1000	4000
Straight Flush	50	100	150	200	250
Four of a Kind	25	50	75	100	125
Full House	9	18	27	36	45
Flush	6	12	18	24	30
Straight	4	8	12	16	20
Three of a Kind	3	6	9	12	15
Two pair	2	4	6	8	10
Jacks or better	1	2	3	4	5

As you travel around Las Vegas you will find many variations of the above pay-off scale. Bars or small clubs, dinner clubs, grocery stores, gas stations and many other locations where you find slots or Video Poker machines, each will have their own variation of the above scale. The above is the best in Las Vegas except, some casinos will give up to $1170 pay-out on the Royal Flush. The other exception is the progressive machines that are in carousels of 8 to 12 machines.

RECOMMENDED PLAY:

Locate in the casino a carousel of machines that have a pay-out for the Royal Flush of over $1500.00 (for 25ᶜ play machines). Remember that the jack-pot starts at $1,000.00 after each pay-out and increases after the deposit of each coin in each machine in the carousel. Most pay-outs for these machines are after they reach $1,500.00. The following recommended play is for 25ᶜ machines. The same strategy applies to other coin machines. Only the pay-outs will differ.

RECOMMENDED PLAY
FOR THE ORIGINAL 5 CARDS:

    1. When dealt - Royal Flush, Straight Flush, 4 of a Kind, Full House, Flush, Straight in first 5 cars, press stand. You have a winner.

    2. Draw 2 cards to any 3 of a Kind. You have a winner.

3. Draw 1 card to any 2 Pair. You have a winner.

4. Draw 3 cards to any Jacks or higher pair. You have a winner.

5. Draw 1 card to any 4 card Straight Flush.

6. Draw 1 card to any 4 card Royal Flush. Yes, even break pairs to draw to the Royal Flush.

7. Draw 1 card to any straight open on either end.

Example: 8 - 9 - 10 - Jack. Either the 7 or Queen will complete your hand.

Drawing to an inside straight will depend on the cards that have been showing.

Example: You have received 7 - 9 - 10 - Jack. You need an eight. If in previous hands you have noticed eights in each hand draw to the eight.

8. Draw 2 cards to a Royal Flush if it has either 3 of the following - Ace, King, Queen, Jack. A matching pair or either of these cards will give you a winning hand. The ten does not win, only Jacks or better.

9. Draw 4 cards to any Jack or higher card.

10. If you have no pairs, no Jack or higher card, draw 5 new cards.

When selecting a seat or machine to play, always notice the amount of the last play. Was it 5 coins, 1 coin or 3 coins. Select the 5 coin machine whenever possible. This means the person who played it last has played the maximum coins and may have built the machine up to a pay-out position in the program of the machine.

GRAND FINALE

Books come, books go, where they stop only the writer knows. This is my wrap-up to what I intend to be, a winning visit to LAS VEGAS by you in fun, gaming, experience and time well spent.

Many people come to LAS VEGAS with the intention of becoming an overnight gaming specialist. Become a big winner, have gifts bestowed on you, see the sights in a limousine, meet the stars in person and go home with a suitcase full of money. Yes, it has happened, but the percent of visitors that it has happened to, is to small to write. Remember gaming is adult play and should be attempted by adults that have studied the game of choice, or have lots of money they want to throw away - give away is a better word selection.

In this busy world of ours, we are looking for a release from the real business, personal and private world we live in. Gambling does take the mind away from these daily problems, but the real world returns after you leave LAS VEGAS. Have your actions in

LAS VEGAS in order, plan your visit, study the games, know where you want to dine, always plan to see the sights, go see the stars in action, and relax in between each of these functions. With this in mind, I have given you a proven way to play each of the games, places to see and excellent places to dine.

LAS VEGAS is one big lighted city; sun-light, search lights, bright lights, street lights, neon lights, star lights, but just don't let these lights blind you to the fact that M O N E Y (green backs) is what keeps these lights bright. The city depends on you coming back, bringing friends, and spending money for their way of life. When you leave, please go with a smile remembering the good times you have had in our city. Be a big winner.

FILE INFORMATION

To each of you who have purchased this book we want to offer you the opportunity to keep abreast of the following information we will offer in the near future. Please fill out the bottom half of this page and return it to our office.

    1. New publications and books we will be offering in the future.

    2. Gaming seminars we will be holding in various cities in the future.

    3. Las Vegas Junkets. We will be offering low cost and sometimes free junkets to Las Vegas in the near future.

By having your name on file you will be offered these services first.

Please return the following information at once.

Name _____ _____   Phone No._____

                                           AC_____

Mail Address _____ _____   City _____

                                           State_____   Zip _____

Purchased book from_____

Yes, I would like to be informed of the following:

    1. New publications or books.

    2. Gaming seminars in my area.

    3. Las Vegas Junkets from my area.

    4. Receive over $100 in Las Vegas Coupons-FREE.

Mail to: either

F & G Concepts
P O Box 18000-226
Las Vegas, Nev. 89109

OR

Please mail to: Parks Publishing Co.

                 P O Box 211

                 Sapulpa, Okla 74067